HOMECOMING
A MEMOIR

GEORGE BALAS

speaks & spells publishing

Canada

ISBN: 0–9781912–0–X

1. Balas, George—Memoirs—Family. 2. Hungary.
I. WWII. II. Nazi occupation. III. Soviet occupation.

Photographs:
Front cover: George at age 6.
Back cover: George at age 70.

Book Design: Susan Hargrove
Cover Design: Kristina Månsson

speaks & spells publishing
A division of Simply4 Communication + Design
293 Malcolm Circle, Dorval, QC. H9S 1T6
T: 514-420-0957 / F: 514-420-0566
www.speaks&spells.ca

Printed in Canada by Lucid Grapics and Printing. www.lucidgp.com

To my children, Christina, Dominique, François and Marc.

To my grandchildren, those present and those to come.

To my wife, Louise, who always believed I had a story to tell them.

To Magi aiè ugr sroreti
a Magararot niutra "ö is
eg Reveue

George

21. Nov 06

Chapter 1

Homecoming

It was September 1963. The fields lay barren and brown after the fall harvest. There wasn't even a tree to break the monotony of the plains stretching as far as the eye could see. Nothing moved but the odd crow crying and picking at the few dry cornstalks.

The last village of Austria disappeared behind us in the haze as we approached the Hungarian border. Louise turned to me and said: "How do you feel?"

"Anxious," I said. "Too many memories."

"Gyurikám, if you want to turn around, I'll understand," she said. "We don't absolutely have to go," and she gently touched my hand on the steering wheel.

"No, no, I won't chicken out now. I must see my home." We drove on silently.

Gradually the road narrowed and weeds appeared through cracks in the pavement. It would have been comforting to see another car heading our way, but there was none. We were alone.

Then, like an ugly scar disfiguring the body of Europe, the Iron Curtain loomed ahead of us. I slowed the car to a halt at the barrier blocking the way. My heart raced crazily as I looked around. Everything was there, just like on that

September day fourteen years before: the watchtowers, the barbed wire fence, the minefields, the searchlights and the machine gun-toting border guards.

Back then I had been on the opposite side of the fence, looking out and yearning to be free. I had risked my life to escape from my country, which had been turned into a gigantic prison by the Communists. Was I a fool to return now for what I hoped would be a short visit?

'Turn back. Turn back, you can still get away!' a voice inside me shouted.

Yet, scared as I was, I decided to stay the course. While we waited to be let in, I had plenty of time to mull over what I had been told the day before at the Canadian embassy in Vienna.

"Sir, if you go back to Hungary, you go at your own risk. They still consider you a citizen of their country. If anything happens to you, we cannot protect you."

"At your own risk, your own risk..." the words drummed in my ears as a soldier on the other side of the rusty gate kept looking at us. I hadn't heard of any refugee who had returned to visit Hungary. I must have been one of the first, and I didn't know what to expect. Without the protection of my newly-acquired Canadian citizenship I felt naked indeed.

But I had to return. After fourteen years I was bursting to see my family again. Many friends and relatives I had loved had already passed away. My father had died three years before and I was prevented by the Communists from being at his bedside to say my last good-bye. But most of all I wanted Louise to meet the family she had married into three years previously. I wanted to show her the house I was born in, the school I went to. I needed to walk with her the streets of my city and the hills of my country. I longed for her to feel and touch the roots of my very being.

We waited on tenterhooks until a soldier finally began cranking a wheel and the border opened. I put the car in gear, and moved it thirty feet forward. Then I heard the gate snap shut behind me.

Suddenly I was gripped by that long-buried fear that all people living in totalitarian systems know so well. Once again I had become a pawn in the hands of people who did not believe in justice. No law could protect me and there was no way of knowing whom I could trust.

Louise passed through controls rapidly. She is a born Canadian. With me they took their time. A garlic-smelling, badly-shaven officer took me to a dingy office and interrogated me for the better half of an hour.

"When did you leave Hungary? How did you do it? Why did you leave? Is our country not good enough for you?"

Obviously wanting to intimidate me, he blew the smoke of his cigarette into my face while cursing in the foulest manner, and there are no fouler curses than those produced in the Hungarian language. After a while I realized I could feel his mood, his insecurity, his anger and, perhaps more than anything else, his envy. He was a Hungarian just like me. But I had made it out. And strangely, the ruder he became, the more my anxiety evaporated.

Something else was changing within me. My long-lasting ambivalence as to where I belonged in this world suddenly left me. As he finally stamped my Canadian passport with a last crude remark, I knew Hungary had ceased to be my home. My roots were here, as were many people I loved deeply, but this was not my country. I didn't belong here anymore.

We took the main highway connecting Vienna and Budapest, the twin capitals of the once-glorious but now defunct Hapsburg Empire. In Austria we had seen Mercedes and BMWs zooming around at mind-boggling speed, but in Hungary chickens, ducks and pigs were the principal users of the road, along with horse-drawn carts that ambled along leisurely under towering loads of hay. After a while I gave up honking and trying to pass. I just relaxed and enjoyed the sweet smell of freshly cut hay.

In villages, women were going to the market with huge baskets on their heads filled with fruits, vegetables, eggs and poultry, just as they had in my childhood. They even seemed to wear the same drab dresses they wore the day I left. The country gave the impression that time had stopped. I felt I was taking a journey into the past in more ways than one.

When we finally entered Budapest, I had trouble containing my excitement. Pointing left and right, I gave running commentary on the surroundings—which bus number went in what direction and which friend or relative used to live where. Then we turned the last corner before reaching my mother's home. I looked up at the street sign hanging crooked from a brick wall and saw graffiti scribbled on it in a childish script: *"Miki szereti Agnest,"* "Nick loves Agnes." I had painted that twenty years before to tease my friend. A world war and a revolution had passed, Stalin and Hitler had come and gone, yet that message was still there. Indeed, very little had changed since I had left. Or so it seemed.

Suddenly we were in front of the house and the whole family was running out, shouting, crying, laughing, hugging and kissing us. A tall young man with a handsome moustache took me in his arms and held me there for a long time repeating over and over, "Welcome home, Gyuri, welcome home."

When he let me loose, I looked into his eyes and softly asked, "Now tell me, who are you?" He smiled as he answered, "Your brother Péter."

"My God, Péter, when I left you were a small boy hardly reaching my belly button, and now you're a full grown man!" We laughed and hugged again and again.

As this emotion-filled day wore on, more cousins, uncles, aunts and never-seen young nieces and nephews kept streaming in to witness the return of the lost sheep. Late in the evening, after cakes and pastry were eaten, coffee and palinka drunk, and a million questions answered, I was totally exhausted. All I wanted was to lie down in my old bed to sleep and dream, but Louise and I could not remain there for the night. Our visitors' visa only allowed us to stay in a hotel reserved for foreigners, where we would be duly registered and informers could keep an eye on us. I was truly an outsider in what had been my country.

During this pilgrimage into my past, the place I most wanted to see was where it all began—the house I grew up in, our family home before the war had forced us out.

This was a huge yellow building sitting in an enormous garden enclosed by a red brick wall. When we got to the wrought-iron gate, I automatically slid my hand through the iron bars searching for the crack in the wall where we used to hide the key. I closed my eyes as my fingers skimmed the rough surface of the bricks and then I felt it, the spot where my brothers and I had poked out a brick years ago.

The moment I found that hole a tidal wave of memories swept me away. When I opened my eyes I didn't see the rust on the gate, the plaster peeling from the house, nor the cement pad where garbage was piled high in dented containers. Miraculously, the gate had opened and regained its shiny black paint. As we walked on, the rose garden, my father's pride and joy, reappeared, as did the tiny stream and waterfall that led to a goldfish pond. As I described this beautiful garden vividly to Louise, all she could see was a field of weeds and overgrown bushes.

We knocked on the front door, not knowing what to expect. A middle-aged woman opened the door, looked at us with a certain mistrust, and told us all the girls were out at school. What girls, I wondered. We were told the house had been converted into a residence for thirty college girls. When I explained to her that this had been my home she invited us in, and let us look around.

Memories kept pouring in as I searched for old souvenirs under layers of surprises. Gone were the oak dining room table and the hand-crafted leather chairs, replaced with gaudy plastic and aluminum furniture. And in what used to be our living-room, instead of the crystal chandelier, now panties, bras and stockings hung from the ceiling to dry.

The high entrance hall, with its twenty-foot-tall stained-glass window that had glowed in a thousand colors in the setting sun, had disappeared. The window had been bricked shut and the hall divided into four rooms full of bunk beds for the girls.

As we poked around in the basement, my eyes fell on a torn wicker chair half-buried under piles of junk. I picked it up, straightened the broken leg and suddenly realized that it was Nanóka's, my paternal grandmother's, armchair I was holding in my hands. As I wiped off the dust and grime I felt Nanóka come alive.

There she was sitting in her chair, her long, snow-white hair combed into a bun on the back of her head. She balanced a pair of tiny steel-rimmed glasses precariously on the tip of her nose while her knitting needles clicked furiously and a woollen sock grew on her lap. She was telling stories—stories of her youth without trains, cars, bicycles, paved roads, electricity or even a kerosene lamp. I hung onto her every word when she told of sleigh rides in winter storms and of starving wolf packs coming out of the woods to chase her horses in a deadly race. She also knew about the glitter and pomp of Emperors, about highway robbers hanged in trees, about mad dogs and wild bulls. I loved Grandmother's stories but I also knew when my bedtime was approaching by the way she let out a sigh and said: "Ah, my dear child, those were the happy days. We didn't have much, but we had time—lots of time to enjoy what the Good Lord had given us." Then she was silent, and I heard only the clicking of needles as I went up to bed.

The house wasn't ours, we rented it from Aunt Margaret. It had been given to her as a wedding present by a doting father. Her husband, a painter, had dedicated his entire life to capturing lions on canvas—lions, lions and more lions everywhere. He even had a big stuffed lion standing on the floor of his studio in the company of wolves, but he painted only the lion.

When her husband died, Aunt Margaret had spread bags of mothballs over his work, locked the studio, moved out, and rented the rest of the house to my parents. Later, when I had learned to pick locks, my brothers Péter, Tamás and I would sneak into those forbidden places, pull off the white sheets covering those ferocious animals and pretend we were Bedouins riding through the sandstorms of Africa.

It was a dream house for artists and children. Its mysteries filled us with myriad fantasies as we hid in its nooks and crannies. The architect, in an apparent attack of grandeur, had attached a four-story-high round tower with narrow slits as windows. We loved to run up and down the spiral staircase with our wooden swords, defending the castle against the enemy of the day. There were balconies, verandas, a wine cellar, a wash cellar, a dark room, chambers for the servants and for the janitor and his family, storage rooms for potatoes and cabbages and a room full of more lion pictures. There was even a basement room where two women sat at a large wooden frame and knotted Persian carpets to my father's design.

But the weirdest thing about this huge house was that it had only two bedrooms. One was for my bigger siblings, while we little ones shared the other bedroom with our parents. Nanóka slept on the sofa in the living room for years, and that was where she later died at the age of ninety-four.

In our old-fashioned household with lots of children, grandparents, cousins and many servants, there was hardly any need for toys. Life was bubbling all the time and we made our own amusements. I remember that, for us children, even laundry day was fun.

Chapter 2

Laundry Day

Laundry was a serious ritual, starting on the evening of every fourth Sunday and lasting until Wednesday afternoon. All the women of the house participated, and Mother hired two additional women just for that occasion. Even Grandmother Nanóka would put away her knitting, leave her comfortable armchair by the window, and pitch in to the frantic activities with relish.

My little brothers Tamás and Péter and I waited with bated breath for the starting gun—the opening of the hamper. This was a huge wooden construction, taller than a grown man and dominating the entire bathroom. It had two doors, the upper one to throw in dirty clothes and the lower one to retrieve the accumulated wash. Its size was a necessity, for it held all the dirty laundry produced by ten of us in a month, even if we did only change clothes once a week after the Saturday bath.

Then Mother called out laughing, "Watch out kids, plug your noses," and swung open the hamper door. The smell was indeed remarkable as the laundry cascaded out like a sulfur-spewing lava flow. The stench got even more powerful as she and the maid sorted underpants here, tablecloths there, until each piece was counted. Then the maid took the piles down to the wash cellar to soak overnight. My brothers and

I could hardly wait for the hamper to be empty to crawl in and build an impenetrable fort that to us smelled of delicious gun smoke.

In the meantime our cook, Mariska Néni, was preparing some caustic solution on the kitchen stove for the next day's wash. How she made this brew I don't know, because she didn't let me into her kitchen on these occasions, no matter how much I begged. "Every year a few children get burned from spilling boiling caustic over themselves," she claimed, and remained firm in spite of my pleading.

The real battle against dirt started at the crack of dawn on Monday morning. By the time I arrived to lend a helping hand, everything was in full swing. A fire was roaring under the big cauldron full of boiling laundry. The steam in the basement was so dense, I could hardly see the two women in bare feet hunched over giant water troughs scrubbing the linen. They always seemed happy to see me. They kissed me, patted me on the head with their chafed red hands and let me stoke the fire and handle the water hose. Being with those women was like being at a beach party.

As soon as a batch of laundry had been scrubbed and rinsed, they carried it up to the attic to dry. The next day, the maid would bring it down in wicker baskets to the dining room to be sprinkled. Why we had to dry the stuff one day and wet it the next was a mystery to me, but it was great fun nonetheless. Mother, Grandmother, my sister, and all the children joined in to spray little driblets of water with our fingers. The adults aimed at the laundry, while my brothers and I preferred squirting each other. There was lots of chatting, laughing and story telling, and of course plenty of gossiping. It was a wonderful way of learning about friends, family and ancestors.

Wednesday was ironing day. In Budapest we used gas-heated irons, far superior to the charcoal-fired ones we had at our summer house. We had also a small electric iron, but this was rarely used since electricity was far too expensive.

The maid and the janitor's wife ironed the finery in the dining room, while in the basement the two laundry women pressed bed sheets, pillow cases, tablecloths, and all the big pieces on a mangle. Our mangle must have been very old, since it was built entirely of wood without any iron at all and the weight pressing down on the rollers was simply a large rock. I loved to sit on this rock, yelling "Faster! Faster!" as the women pushed it back and forth. It was just like being on a swing, and the tales these women told were incredibly fascinating. They talked of men and all the strange things they did with them. Of course, I didn't believe half of their stories because I knew babies were brought by the stork.

Things quieted down by the evening of the fourth day. Mother counted, stored and locked up the linen. The laundry women were paid and went away to return again four weeks later. The maid dressed once more in her black and white uniform to serve at the table. In the morning she would return to dusting, sweeping, waxing the floor, and polishing brass and silver as usual. When Father reappeared I knew the laundry ceremony had come to its end. But the next exciting activity was usually just around the corner.

Chapter 3

The Pig

Inside the home, women ruled and did the work. The kingdom of men was beyond the four walls, where they could do as they pleased, as long as they didn't drag dirt into the house. Once, however, the men of my family trespassed on this unwritten law—did they ever! It had to do with a pig.

In preparing for the winter food supply, Father usually ordered half a hog from the butcher. It came already cleaned and cut into pieces so that the messy work was done away from home. Once the meat arrived, it was the women's task to prepare a variety of sausages, hams and other meat dishes that were either pickled in a wooden barrel or hung in the chimney for smoking.

One year my brother-in-law questioned the economics of the whole process. "We shouldn't pay good money to the butcher," he said. "We should buy a live pig from the farmer and do the butchering ourselves." He soon convinced my older brother Jancsi of the soundness of his idea. Our janitor also offered to lend a hand, hoping that a few sausages would be his reward. It was more difficult to get my father's permission. Father had been born and raised on a farm and knew that the laundry room in the basement of a city house was not the best place to slaughter a pig. He had some doubts about the ability of the men as well. In the end, however, he gave his permission, overruling Mother, who objected vehemently to a live pig invading her house.

The pig arrived on a rainy November afternoon. It seemed quite content riding in the farmer's horse cart on a thick bed of straw, until these three musketeers began pushing it out. The moment the pig hit the street, it gave a loud squeal, knocked over its tormentors and ran for its life. It was an enormous beast, heavier than the three men together, but it could run and dodge with amazing agility. The farmer was bent over laughing as he watched men and beast tackling and wrestling each other to the ground. Finally, after a valiant struggle, the pig conceded defeat and was led to the laundry room, where a fire burned under the cauldron and a couple of shiny butcher knives were laid out.

I climbed up to the top of the mangle for a better view of the action. From all the head-scratching going on, I knew I would soon witness quite a show.

"This isn't a pig, this is a monster," said the janitor in a shaken voice.

"You did say you had butchered pigs before, didn't you?" replied my brother-in-law, a university professor.

"I have, but this is a hippopotamus. I don't even know how I'll get the knife into this animal."

"Maybe if we turned him on his back you could reach his throat easier," Jancsi suggested helpfully.

They all agreed this was a brilliant idea, and immediately swung into action, grabbing and twisting all four of the animal's legs. The pitch of squealing reached an octave higher, but the stubborn pig refused to turn on its back, emptying every orifice of its trembling body onto the floor. The men were even more determined to succeed. With enormous twists and pushes they managed to turn the pig for a moment, then Jancsi threw himself on its belly, and as somebody shouted "Now!" the janitor thrust the knife into its exposed throat.

The squealing became ear-shattering. The pig, refusing to die, gave a formidable kick and knocked all of them to the blood-soaked floor. With blood gushing all over, it ran out of the laundry room, through a long corridor and into the garden. We all ran after it, but as I cleared the door my Nanny caught me by the arm and dragged me upstairs and into the bathtub. I could scream louder than the pig, but for me the show was over.

Next morning, when I went down to inspect the scene, three women were scrubbing blood and excrement off the floor, walls and windows of the entire stinking basement. I didn't see any men around. But of course, cleaning inside the house was a woman's job.

Chapter 4

The Toy

We called our nice old family doctor, Bandy Bácsi—a very respectful and endearing way of addressing an older Hungarian gentleman. Whenever he came to see one of us children suffering from colds, measles or other assorted illnesses, it was a lengthy affair. He always spent a long time chatting with my parents, and over time they became friends. I liked his visits as well. He was funny and kind and never scared or hurt us children. I also enjoyed going to his office. There was a wonderful sweet smell of medicine mixed with the aroma of freshly baked cookies wafting over from the kitchen, and when Bandy Bácsi was finished with us, his wife, Marta Néni, rushed in and stuffed us full with her delicious cookies. I have never met a more delightful medical team.

Bandy Bácsi was a conscientious doctor. He practiced state-of-the-art medicine, the art of the early 1930s. In those days, everybody was convinced it was healthy for children to be taken high into the Alps, where the pure mountain air would do marvels. Bandy Bácsi was able to persuade my parents of this without any great effort.

At that time we were five children in the family and, with the exception of my older brother, we all had minor health problems. Nothing serious, but my parents wanted to do the best for us and so, one by one, we were sent to the finest sanatoriums in Austria or Switzerland for six months to a year. This was a tremendous financial sacrifice on their part, even though my father's business affairs were going well during those years.

At age six, I was a skinny boy, a bit cross-eyed, but that didn't reduce my *joie de vivre* at all. Aside from being skinny, there was nothing wrong with my health.

Nevertheless, late in the summer of 1935, at the end of our family vacation in Austria, Mother took me on a long bus ride up into the mountains. The road twisted and turned over clear running streams, through dark pine forests and meadows where cows grazed the last flowers of summer. It was peaceful and quiet. The other passengers were dozing off. They had seen the snowy peaks and heard the cowbells before. I was alone looking out the window, pressing my nose against the glass, not so much to admire the beauty of the mountains, but to hide my anxiety about the purpose of this journey.

At each village a few passengers got off the bus, until only the two of us were left traveling higher and higher up the mountain. Finally the last curve was negotiated and there stood an immense building, the sanatorium of Stolzalpe. The entire grey building was surrounded by a huge open-air balcony where dozens of boys were already lying in their beds, dressed in pyjamas with blankets pulled up to their ears. What a strange thing to do so early in the afternoon, I thought. Why aren't they climbing trees or trampling in mud puddles like normal boys? For someone just over the age of six this was a very disturbing question.

A buxom matron helped Mother change me into pyjamas, both of them doing their best to calm my mounting fears, but without much success. Soon I was out on the balcony in bed with all the other children, who raised their heads to inspect the new inmate. *"Kinder schoen ruhig im Bett bleiben, bitte,"* called the Matron in a friendly but strange and unintelligible language. Everybody else must have understood her, since the little heads quickly returned to their pillows.

Mother sat down beside my bed, caressed my face softly and pulled a present from her purse. As I tore off the wrapping, full of anticipation, my anxieties ebbed away. It was a lovely little toy. Its long wooden frame was painted yellow with black triangles and, stretched over it on a fuzzy leather belt, a mouse, a cat and a dog chased each other with a squeaky sound as I turned a crank. Oh, isn't it cute, I thought. Will the cat catch the mouse if I spin it fast enough? Let's try! Faster, crank faster, the cat is almost there, faster! 'Look, Mummy, look, look how they run, look, look!'

When I lifted my head, her chair was empty. My mother had gone. She had left me alone in this alien world.

The toy slipped from my hand and crashed to the floor, taking all my emotions along with it. I never touched that cursed toy again. Whether I cried, I don't remember. I hardly remember a thing from the time my mother left me until my father came to pick me up nine months later.

Only two short events were powerful enough to pierce through the fog of amnesia.

My appendectomy was one. Anesthetics still being primitive and dangerous, it may have been that the doctor was overly cautious in administering the drug. As his knife sliced the skin of my belly, I was still conscious. It felt as if a lion were tearing out my insides—a huge male lion with a big bushy mane and enormous white teeth. Its roar was deafening, or was it my desperate scream that I can still hear from the distance of seven decades? My parents didn't come; they were informed too late.

Later, much later, my sister, Zsuzsi, and her husband came by on their honeymoon. This was the second event I can still recall. Again, I was out on the balcony, in bed, wearing light blue pyjamas. I didn't know what to say to my beloved sister, who suddenly appeared as a married woman. I wanted to shout, 'take me home, take me home,' but no sound came from my throat. She chatted and smiled, and as they were leaving she gave me a present. This time I didn't even open the gift. I just pulled the blanket of amnesia tighter over my head.

Obviously, we boys weren't in bed all the time; we must have also played outside, but I have no recollection of that. We must have received school instruction as well, since sixty years later, going through Mother's old souvenirs, I found a letter I wrote from the sanatorium in German. Someone must have taught me that strange language. Someone must have taught me to read and write, but who, how and when?

The events around me I could erase from memory, but not my feelings.

After my mother disappeared, an immense loneliness overcame me. I was desperately homesick. I was abandoned, helpless, unloved. How I longed to be taken in her arms, to be kissed and caressed. But where was she?

Slowly, as the months wore on, my feelings changed and eventually determination took the place of desperation. It must have been sometime after spring returned that I resolved to go home. I started to plan my escape, spending many hours thinking and dreaming about how I would travel, hide, eat and drink. I am convinced that, had my father not come for me just a little later, somebody might have found a little boy walking in his blue pyjamas through the woods of Austria in the direction of Hungary. I am also convinced he would have tried and tried again until he reached his home.

Stolzalpe was more of a prison than a sanatorium to me. It must have been there that the will to flee from miserable situations became so deeply ingrained in my character. Without this experience, possibly I would not have escaped prison camp, police custody, bad jobs and dozens of other wretched conditions later in life, with such apparent ease.

There were other strange consequences to this painful

period. I became frightened when people gave me gifts. I panicked every time the woman I loved gave me a present. Why does she want to leave me? What did I do that she must abandon me? Why does she do this to me? Why? Finding no answer, I became angry and wanted to hit and hurt. A long time passed and many hurtful events took place before I discovered deep in my memory the haunting ghost of that abandoned little boy with the mouse, the cat and the dog.

When I returned home from Austria, our dear old Bandy Bácsi performed a check-up on me and found to his surprise that I was not an ounce fatter than before my exile. He tried all the tricks of the medical trade, but I remained skinny as a stick for a long while.

Bandy Bácsi and Marta Néni remained good friends of our family for many years. Then one day, towards the end of the war, we heard the horrible news: together they had committed suicide. They wanted to die in their own home, rather than at Auschwitz.

Chapter 5

My First Business Ventures

I was sitting in the tub all alone, happy that I didn't have to share the bath with my two little brothers anymore. Suddenly, at the mature age of seven, I was feeling very grown up.

Splashing around merrily, I kept squeezing the slippery soap, making it jump. It became smaller and smaller, until I pitched the useless sliver into the garbage. That moment, in a flash, I glimpsed the first business opportunity of my life. Why throw away all the little pieces? I could collect the leftovers, boil them in a pot and when the goo was thick enough, press them into a solid form. Surely people would be delighted to buy recycled soap. Excited, I climbed out of the bathtub and immediately began laying the foundations of my future business empire.

From then on, no soap was safe in the house. The moment I spotted a slightly used piece, it would disappear into a cooking pot I had smuggled out of the kitchen. My factory was in the corner of our bathroom. There, on a little table, stood a gas burner that Father used every morning to heat water for shaving. This burner was ideal for my purpose as well.

Soon I was cooking the first batch. The stuff bubbled and smoked, but refused to solidify. Before the whole lot turned completely black, I quickly changed my business plan. Instead of making hard cakes, I would sell it as liquid soap in little paper containers. This turned out to be a lovely product. Its brown color was remarkable and its fragrance unique. My parents, aunts and uncles loved the merchandise. I could see it in their smiles as they forked over the purchase price, the equivalent of five cents a cup.

I savored the sound of coins jingling in my pocket. The excitement of having my own money was delicious. My parents believed one shouldn't just give a child money, not even pocket money, because if he was old enough to spend it, he was old enough to earn it.

Encouraged by my business fortune, I was cooking another batch, when a little accident happened. As I stirred the brew faster and faster, the pot suddenly jumped off the burner, spilling the slippery goo all over the bathroom floor. For one moment I was petrified, but the next I was on my knees wiping up the mess, using roll after roll of toilet paper. When I was finished, everything looked clean and orderly to my eyes.

Next morning, I heard Father happily whistling his favorite opera arias while sitting in the tub. Suddenly there was a crash, a thud, and the sound of ripping cloth. I froze, sure that something really bad had happened. Luckily, he hadn't hurt himself as he stepped on the soapy floor with wet feet and fell, tearing off the shower curtain in the process

I was surprised Father wasn't angry with me. Perhaps he was secretly proud of his little son's first business venture. Nevertheless, he closed my lucrative enterprise, invoking *force majeure.*

Now this was a serious business problem. My sole source of cash had disappeared in a flash. I was discouraged for a day or two, but soon dreamed up another venture. I would recycle leftover candle stumps.

Again, my factory was in the corner of the bathroom,

over the gas burner. Thick thread from Grandmother's knitting became the perfect wick material and forgotten candle stumps could be found in dusty cupboards. I had only to melt the wax in a pot over the flame, pour it into a rolled-up paper tube, and a new candle would be ready for the captive family market. My previous customers returned and were just as pleased to buy the new product as they had been with the soap.

Unfortunately, soon after this auspicious beginning, there was another incident. Again that restless pot became independent, jumped off the burner and spilled molten wax over the floor. But this time things were more serious. In a moment I had a roaring fire on my hands! When the flames reached my father's nightshirt hanging nearby, it lit up like a torch. I wanted to scream for help, but couldn't. I was frozen with fear. I don't know how long I stared at the flames before I finally grabbed the chamber pot from under the table and poured gallons of water over the blaze, until half the Danube was flowing between my feet.

Slowly, water gained the upper hand over fire. The last flame died with an angry hiss, leaving me trembling among the ruins. The bathroom was a mess and the charred, soggy nightshirt was beyond repair.

When Father inspected the scene that evening, I knew immediately that I had stretched paternal tolerance beyond the breaking point. There was no sign of a benevolent smile anymore. He didn't mete out any punishment for my foolishness, but his words were enough to convince me that the little gas burner and I had to part company forever.

It took me a couple of days to recover from this unfortunate setback, but once the bug of entrepreneurship bites you, you are in business for good. I must have been bitten viciously, because hardly a week passed before my next project was underway. It was to be a cigarette factory.

In those days many people rolled their own cigarettes to save money. They bought finely chopped tobacco and stuffed it into little paper tubes. My revolutionary idea was to substitute expensive virgin tobacco with tobacco left in cigarette butts.

This seemed a brilliant plan, and I immediately set to work recycling the contents of ashtrays. Customers would get their money's worth of nicotine and there would be no extra charge for the bacteria. A fantastic deal by anybody's standard. I had no difficulty producing the cigarettes and they really looked good—they were firm and exuded a powerful aroma. But there was a problem with the clients. This time they didn't smile nor did they open their purses, even as I lowered the price. They looked rather as if their stomachs were ready to turn when the smell of the cigarettes reached their nostrils. No question, I was facing the first serious marketing problem of my life.

Luckily, I found a business partner in the son of our janitor. He was a couple of years older and he was allowed to go out on the street to play football and do more or less whatever he wanted. For a fair commission he was not only willing to sell the cigarettes on the street, but would also pick up from the sidewalk an unlimited supply of butts for me. From then on business was good and my little piggy bank got generously fed.

Chapter 6

My Parents

My parents' childhoods were like night and day. Father was born in July 1888, six months after his father, Péter Breining, had died unexpectedly from pneumonia at the age of forty-seven. Grandfather's legacy was minuscule, a pocket watch, a few leather-bound books and a tiny pension. But Grandmother Nanóka was a resourceful woman. She saved, struggled, and didn't rest until Father had finished his schooling and graduated a mechanical engineer.

"We led a very modest life," she told me many years later. "We didn't have money for concerts, and yet your father loved opera so much. Luckily, he had a good voice and he sang his favorite arias so beautifully. He was happy singing and whistling, even with his pockets empty."

Mária, my mother, on the other hand, entered this world wrapped in luxury. Grandfather Johan, a well-known doctor, could afford to keep his family in great comfort. He was the first person in Pécs to purchase an automobile and his house was the first to be lit by electricity. The fact that his wife, whom we called Nagymami, inherited her family's soap factory was surely an added benefit. They lived in the center of town in an old monastery that had been converted into an elegant residence. They escaped the summer heat in their mountain villa overlooking the city and spent September at their vineyard. Winter was the season for glittering balls, theater, music and opera.

Mother often told us how Nagymami would spoil her by a thousand little gestures, not least by sending the maid to her bedside with exquisite breakfasts. Luckily Grandfather Johan didn't want wealth to go to his children's heads. His little daughter could enjoy fancy breakfasts in bed, but by eight o'clock she had to be downstairs to receive her tutor. If she was even just one minute late, there was hell to be paid. Making the teacher wait would have been disrespectful and Grandfather insisted that everyone, even the lowest servant, be treated with respect.

For entertainment, nothing could compete with music in their home. Nagymami and Mother played the piano, her brothers, Hugo and Béla, the violin, Victor the cello and Grandfather the bass. The love of music stayed with all of them throughout their lives.

Just as my parents' backgrounds were worlds apart, so were their temperaments. Father was an enterprising spirit, always ready to try new things. Curious throughout his life, he wanted to understand how things worked, and could hardly wait to tell us about his latest discoveries. I remember when I was nine or ten he tried to explain to me atomic physics, relativity, and a host of other mysterious things.

He had a great sense of humor, joking and teasing us with a passion. At the same time, he had a short temper, and a slight irritation could send him into a rage or a week-long sulking silence. On these stormy occasions, Mother's soothing calm was a blessing. She never raised her voice.

Father had faith in humanity almost to a fault. He couldn't imagine that anyone he knew would lie, cheat or act from pure self-interest. Mother was more of a realist. She had an uncanny ability to size people up, and could almost see through them. When Father was too trusting or naïve she warned him, but often he didn't listen.

An early photograph of my father as a naval officer in the Austro-Hungarian Navy shows a tall, strongly built man with black hair and eyes that look straight into yours—the confident picture of a handsome young man with a strong personality and determination.

Mother, judging by her early pictures, was an attractive young woman, although perhaps not what people would call a raving beauty. From her soft, gentle smile and almost dreamy look in these photos, one would never guess the enormous strength of character and quiet wisdom that, combined with kindness, were the hallmarks of her personality.

My parents met through my father's good friend Béla Johan, my mother's eldest brother. Soon afterward, they began planning their wedding, but first Father changed his name. He was born Pál Breining, the family name of his paternal ancestors who had immigrated from Germany two centuries before. It had become quite common for people, after so many years in Hungary, to drop their original name for a Hungarian-sounding one. It may also be that, since Father had never known his own father, he was less attached to family tradition. Why he chose the surname Balázs from the thousands of other possibilities I shall never know; I never thought to ask.

For their honeymoon, they rented a quiet hotel room overlooking the center of Sarajevo, where they planned to stay a few weeks. They had just finished unpacking when Mother suddenly had an uneasy feeling that something was seriously wrong with Grandfather. There were no telephones, and she became desperate. To ease her fears, Father repacked the suitcases, paid the hotel, and they returned home. When they arrived, Grandfather was in a coma and had already received the last rites. He recovered this time but died soon thereafter of the Spanish flu. Mother couldn't explain her premonition. "I just knew something was wrong," she said. This was not the first time she showed her uncanny intuition, nor the last.

Meanwhile, fate had played another trick on them. Had they stayed just a few more days in the hotel, they would have heard the pistol shot that killed the Austrian crown-prince and ignited the First World War. That murder also ruined my father's dream of studying in England for a year. He already had tickets for both of them in his pocket. Instead, he was ordered to work in a munitions factory in Vienna for the duration of the war. He couldn't go back to the Navy, because the British had quite unceremoniously sunk the entire Austro-Hungarian Navy, and thus Father, along with thousands of other seamen, became a landlubber.

It was a long and devastating war, until then the most murderous in human history. But even when a cease-fire was finally signed after four long years, Hungary's suffering didn't end. A communist revolution broke out in the country that created almost more havoc than the war itself.

For a while it was touch and go whether Hungary would become a Soviet-style dictatorship like Russia. Lynchings, hangings and shootings were commonplace, and it became almost impossible to buy food. Father and Mother had to go out of the city to scrounge through the fields for potatoes the farmers might have missed in the harvest. This was quite a change for a young woman who not so long before had lived in luxury. But Mother didn't complain. As a matter of fact, I never heard her utter a single complaint in my entire life.

After a year of utter chaos, the communist revolution came to an end when Admiral Horthy rode into Budapest at the head of his rag-tag army. With order returned, people went back to work and a peaceful existence.

For a year or two, Father taught in a technical school, but soon was hired as plant manager in a textile factory. He saved every penny from his salary and after a couple of years he quit, bought a few weaving machines, rented a basement and started his business. Mother gave enthusiastic support to this venture, and in the evenings, after tucking her two young children—Zsuzsi, six, and Jancsi, five—into bed, she would join him weaving.

Their hard work paid off. Ten years later, Father had a new factory employing well over one hundred people. Then one day his cousin, Andor Márkus, offered to invest in the business. He had just inherited a large sum of money and didn't know what to do with it.

When Father explained his cousin's proposal to Mother, I was playing quietly behind their sofa and heard every word.

"Andor would invest a huge amount," he said. "I could double production, open up new markets, export to the Balkans, and create more jobs. Think of the money we could earn. This is a fantastic opportunity I'm going to grab it."

Mother listened quietly and, after a long pause, replied: "These aren't your words, Pali. I hear Andor speaking through you. You never showed that much interest in money. You were always more interested in seeing whether an idea of yours could be realized. That's why you worked so hard and took the risks. And that's why you still have so much fun with it. Andor has such a different character from yours. You wouldn't get along for long. Don't let him take over your business."

"But you don't understand. He wouldn't take it over, he would get only a half share of the business. Isn't that a fair proposal?"

"You may be right," Mother said. "This could be a fair offer. But even then, I don't think you should do it."

Next day at dinner, Father was elated as he told us he had a new partner. He described in glowing terms the wonderful things Andor and he would do together. Mother seemed to listen as intently as the rest of us. Whatever thoughts were behind her smile, she didn't share them with us.

For a few weeks Father was in heaven, but slowly he became more withdrawn. His mood gradually soured and my brothers and I avoided him whenever we could. Finally, after a year, he couldn't take the mounting tension between Andor and himself. He sold his entire business to his cousin. Then, freed from stress, he relaxed and started joking again.

Suddenly he had a fortune in his hands and no clear plan for what to do with it. So, just like anywhere else in the world, when promoters smell a lot of money they buzz to it with business proposals like bees to the honey pot. And they swarmed around Father for a long time, until finally one stung him.

One evening, as was their habit, my parents sat on their bedroom balcony discussing the events of the day. I shared this room with them, and if I wasn't asleep and perked up my ears, I could hear most of what they were saying. That night Father talked about his decision to start an automobile factory.

"You know I've had several meetings with Mr. Fejes," he said, "and I'm convinced he's an excellent automobile engineer. But he needs capital to build a factory and production lines. I'll do the financing, and together we'll build the first car manufacturing company in Hungary."

Hearing this unexpected news, Mother must have taken several deep breaths, because it was a while before she replied.

"I've met Mr. Fejes. I can't judge his engineering skills, but he's certainly a big talker. He seems far too sure of himself. He thinks he can do anything. I wouldn't trust that man. Besides, what do you know about cars?"

"Not much," replied Father, "but look, those two Germans, Daimler and Benz, joined together and became so successful. Or how about the two English fellows, Rolls and Royce, one an engineer, the other a financier? They did the same thing we want to do."

"Palikám," Mother interrupted, "why don't you stay with what you know? You're the greatest expert in the country in textiles. You know everything about spinning, weaving and dyeing the fabric. You have an uncanny talent for anticipating trends in women's wear. Please, stay with what you know. This car business looks thrilling but it could ruin us."

As I listened to them, I hoped Mother's pleading would fall on deaf ears. I wanted to urge him on 'Go Father, go! You can do it!' as I was all excited at the prospect of shiny new cars popping out of the factory by the hundreds. Perhaps I could even race them one day. Father must have heard my silent prayer, for he did join Mr. Fejes and they started building cars.

My brother, Jancsi, who was twenty-one at the time, was allowed to take the cars for a test drive. To my great delight, he often took me along. I enjoyed the admiring looks of people as we sped along the broad avenues. Our cars were special. While Mr. Ford was still building nothing but his Model Ts that looked like a black shoebox on wheels, ours had a more modern style. Aerodynamically shaped like today's hatchbacks, with recessed door handles and a lightweight motor, the design was in many respects years ahead of its time. And to top it all off, you could get a car in any color you desired.

Unfortunately the engines drank oil like crazy.

It took a long time to find the cause of this ticklish problem, and before it could be resolved, Father's money ran out. As with all our family catastrophes, this one, too, visited us at the dinner table.

The mood had been growing gloomy over the last few weeks and we were eating our soup in silence, when the maid handed Father a telegram. We all looked at him anxiously as he tore it open and read it. His jaw tightened. For a while he just gazed at nothing. Then he flung his chair back, threw his napkin on the table, and stormed out of the room.

Frightened, we turned our eyes to Mother. She carefully folded her linen napkin, rolled it up tightly and pulled it through a silver ring as she always did after the meals. She looked at us calmly and said in an unhurried tone, "Children, you stay at the table and finish your meal. Juliska will serve you peach cake for desert. I'll be back shortly." Then she followed Father.

We hadn't yet finished dessert when she returned. "I have news for you children. Tomorrow we'll take the train to Pécs, to Nagymami's vineyard. We'll stay with her for awhile. You'll have lots of fun helping with the wine harvest."

"And the cars?" we asked in unison.

"There will be no more cars. It's finished. We're bankrupt." She spoke so quietly we could hardly hear and even less understand what she meant.

Like so many other things he did well in his life, Father lost his fortune with dignity. He had not hidden money under Mother's name, nor stashed a pile away in a Swiss bank account. He was simply and honestly broke. He didn't even have a penny left to buy food for the family, and so, after twenty-two years of marriage, Mother had to take her children back to her own mother. Still, she never complained.

Nor did I. At age ten, climbing fruit trees and stuffing myself full of peaches and figs was a heck of a lot more fun than sitting motionless on a school bench, arms properly folded while painfully pretending interest in the teacher's mathematical contortions. There was no school in the world that could match the fun of making wine, trampling around in a huge wooden vat with bare feet, knee-deep in juicy grapes.

Six weeks passed in a flash. One morning, Mother came into our room, hugged each of us, and sang "Hooray! Father has a job. He sent money for the train. We can go home."

This time Father had listened to Mother's advice and had taken a position as managing director of a large textile mill. When we entered our home everybody was back, even the cook, the maid and our nanny.

With my parents' ordeal over, peace and prosperity descended again on the family. Father was in a business he really knew and had time again to pursue his passion of nature hiking. On Sunday mornings, after Mass, he would often take me along into the hills of Buda. I liked these excursions, full of easy banter and without the usual comments about my dismal high-school results.

Our favorite spot was on top of Hármas Határ mountain, a good place to spread out a blanket, enjoy our sandwiches and watch the local gliding club teach young men to fly in the valley below.

Huffing and puffing, a dozen air-cadets dragged the engineless glider up the slopes. Once the plane was in position and its tail firmly secured to a ground peg, they strapped a student to the wooden seat and hitched a heavy rubber cord to the nose of the aircraft. Then, pulling the rope, they ran downhill like a bunch of screaming devils in search of hellfire. When the elastic reached its limit, the fellow in the back released the tail, the pilot's head jerked back, and the glider shot forward like a slingshot. Relieved from the pull of the rubber, the men on the ground lost their balance and rolled down the hill in a ball of flailing arms and legs almost as fast as the airplane. A flight of a few hundred meters was what they usually achieved, but occasionally a pilot would catch an updraft and soar around in majestic silence for a minute or two.

"It must be such a pleasure to fly," Father sighed. "How I would like to see the world from above."

"Are you dreaming of an aircraft factory?" I asked. "It would be easy. A few sticks of wood, a sheet of canvas and you'd be in business," I added, convinced there was nothing in the world my father couldn't do.

"No, no, my dear. I've learned my lesson with the car factory. From now on I'll stick to what I know." He laughed, and after a while added,

"You know, my automobile venture wasn't so farfetched. Four years ago when I got seduced by that business, dozens of mechanics and engineers were jostling to catch the future wave of transportation. Packard, Porsche, Austin, Bugatti, Nash, Chrysler, Studebaker were all individual entrepreneurs. Now it seems a few large corporations will gobble up the entire automotive industry. In those days, you didn't need millions to start a car factory. I think I had almost enough to succeed, but we were too slow fixing the lubrication problem."

"Do you regret going into the car business?" I asked hesitantly, afraid of stirring up painful memories.

"No, not at all! You should never regret the past. That's a waste of time. Look carefully and you'll find something good in even the worst calamity. Use your mistakes to learn lessons for the future."

"And what did you learn that was worth your entire fortune?" I asked with tongue in cheek.

"To trust your mother's great wisdom," Father replied, and his face lit up in a smile. "But we'd better go. She wanted an early supper tonight."

On the way home Father continued. "You know, in my youth the automobile was the wave of the future, and in your life, it's the airplane. Who knows, maybe you'll produce these flying machines by the dozens."

"I don't think so, Father. I like boats better. I want to build a boat to sail across the ocean. That's my dream."

"Well, where there's a will, there's a way. Stick to it and you'll succeed," he said, and we talked of boats and ships all the way home.

Those two years following the bankruptcy were quiet years and possibly the longest period in my parents' married life without major upheavals. But it was a short lull in the storm, for in the distance one could almost hear the next war approaching.

Chapter 7

Boat Building

Where did my love of boats, water and the sea come from? I don't know. Saltwater spray had never touched my face and yet as a young boy I already dreamed of sailing the oceans. It could have come from my father. An ex-officer in the Austro-Hungarian Navy, he enjoyed water like a frog. He would jump into every river, lake or pool whenever he saw one and, long before I was born, he already had a motorboat, one of the first on the Danube.

Then I heard the stories about Uncle Kaufman that excited my fantasy. At the age of eighteen he ran away from home, landed in England, changed his name to Kenedi and was hired on as seaman on a British merchant vessel. It didn't take long before he was captain of the ship, putting into every port of the world. The tales he told about storms, cannibals, pirates, icebergs and sea monsters made me restless. At the age of seven or eight I was dying to follow in his wake and be captain of my own ship.

While I listened to all these stories, the object of my dream lay hidden on the shores of Lake Balaton. The next summer, as I was nosing around the local boatyard with my friend, Zebi, I spotted something under a willow tree, almost hidden in the high grass. It was a small rowboat. She seemed to be in her final resting place, rotting away peacefully. She must have shed her last coat of paint years before. Now snails and frogs made their home among her decaying planks. Yet to me she looked beautiful. She had potential.

So we bought her for a few coins, dragged her home and began reconstruction. The plan was to nail a cloth to the planks, then smear a thick coat of tar over the entire surface to render it watertight.

We had no problem finding tar. The road in front of our house had been resurfaced that day and the asphalt was still warm. It was easy to scrape off buckets full of the black gooey stuff.

Finding a big enough cloth to stretch over our entire boat was a bigger challenge. We snuck into the house when Mother wasn't around and checked out her linen cupboard. There was a very fine lace tablecloth she used often, so we skipped over that one. Anyway it was useless for our purpose, too flimsy, too many little holes in the lacework. After discarding a pile of fancy items we finally found the perfect material at the bottom of the cupboard. Wrapped in tissue paper and tied up with a pink ribbon was a heavy tablecloth embroidered with many colourful flowers. I knew Mother didn't like it, since I had never seen her use it. I was sure she wouldn't miss it.

We slit the cloth with Father's garden shears, nailed it to the hull, then cut off the corners, hammered in a couple more nails and snipped off a bit again, all this time smearing on thicker and thicker blobs of tar with spoons, knives and fingers. We were as black as the boat when the time for launching arrived. Apart from the whites of our eyes, everything around us was pitch black, our clothes, the tools, the grass and even the sand of the beach. But we were happy and the ship floated.

Well, long enough at least for us to jump in and paddle around for a few minutes. We were still afloat when Mother came out for a dip in the lake. Seeing us, she burst out laughing.

"Good job, boys. Congratulations. How did you do it?"

Then before we could satisfy her curiosity, she stepped closer and with a finger cautiously touched a yellow flower still uncovered by tar. Her smile disappeared as she found more flowers carelessly left bare.

"Oh, my God. This can't be true," She gasped. "My most precious wedding present. I never used it; I was so afraid it could get spoiled. It was so beautiful. How could you do this?"

She looked at me without another word, and slowly tears began rolling down her cheeks. She just kept looking at me in silence. Then she turned and went back into the house. Her quiet sorrow hurt me more than any punishment I could have received. I had no more pleasure in the boat. We dragged it back to the boatyard and dumped it under the willow tree.

For awhile after that, my boat building urge remained dormant, but not for very long. I must have been in my early teens when one day in Budapest I gazed out of our living room window towards the west and wondered what lay beyond the hills I could see. Some other hills, I thought, and beyond those, more hills and mountains and lakes, and beyond those the ocean and finally America. I closed my eyes to better feel the ocean and its moods, its calms and storms, its roaring waves. If one built a boat sturdy enough, one could cross the seas safely even in the smallest of boats, I imagined, like a corked bottle can float safely through the fiercest storms. Yes! One day I would build that boat and sail to America.

I had to design my boat right then and there. To do it full life-size, my drafting board had to be huge. So I grabbed a chalk, ran down to our dead-end street and began sketching on the pavement. As the outlines of the boat slowly emerged with the layout of the galley, the bunks and the cockpit, I could almost feel the boat starting to surge through the waves. It was some thirty years later that I launched my last boat, my favorite, but she would be the one to resemble that childhood sketch the most. It is *Anahita* that took me over all the oceans of the world, and that I am still sailing with so much pleasure today.

Chapter 8

The War Begins

A year or so after Adolph Hitler became chancellor, Father went to Germany on a business trip. Returning home, he was full of praise for the changes he had observed. "It's amazing how Hitler turned chaos into order in just one year. No more armed gangs roaming the streets," he said. "Unemployment is finished, everyone is working. The place is booming. You should see the Autobahn. There's not a single road crossing it! It's absolutely mind-boggling. And look at this miniature camera, isn't this fantastic workmanship? I bought it for you," and he handed me a camera not much bigger than a man's thumb.

Mother waited for a lull in his whirlwind of enthusiasm before she spoke.

"Well, I don't know. Hitler has done great things for Germany until now, I must admit, yet I'm worried. That man has something in his eyes, in his voice, in his speech that frightens me. He may grab more power and then God knows what he may do."

"Ah! Here you go again with your intuition," Father interjected. "Look at the facts. Hitler was elected democratically. All his power was bestowed on him legally by the president. He won't take power illegally."

"But what about his book? You read his *Mein Kampf.* You know what he's aiming at. Even just half of it would be a catastrophe."

"He wrote that nonsense while still young, sitting in jail," Father said. "You should forget it. People mature with responsibility. He's now a Head of State. There are many people in England and America who admire him for his achievements, like Charles Lindbergh and Henry Ford. Even some English newspapers praise him for standing up to the communists."

"I hope you're right." Mother sighed, and the discussion turned to more mundane subjects.

Father was so impressed by the social and economic advances he saw in Germany that he decided to support similar efforts in our country. When a struggling newspaper editor approached him with a proposal to launch a daily that would promote industry and greater equality, Father agreed to finance the venture. The paper was named *Virradat—* *"Awakening"* in Hungarian and Father became its publisher. He even designed its logo.

But soon disturbing news began to flood out of Germany, rapidly washing away Father's enthusiasm. Political opponents of the Nazis disappeared one by one, inmates of mental hospitals died mysteriously and a host of anti-Semitic laws were declared. At first these laws were more annoying than damaging, like the one prohibiting Jews from employing Christian household help. But soon mixed marriages became outlawed and Jewish university professors and civil servants were dismissed.

"This is unfair! This is stupid!" Father burst out. "Some of the brightest brains in Germany are Jewish. They will emigrate. Why chase them away? I think Hitler is losing his mind."

My father's association with the newspaper didn't last long either. He became increasingly annoyed as the editor began to support the Hungarian Nazi Party. One morning when

Father had stayed in bed with a nasty cold, I brought him the latest edition of the news. "Jew, get out of Hungary!" screamed the headline in huge black letters. For a moment he glared at it, then threw the paper to the floor and ordered, "Bring me the phone."

He dialed, spoke a few heated words and slammed down the receiver. "So, that's it. It's finished. I'm not going to support that filthy rag anymore." The paper's circulation nevertheless increased under a new publisher and soon it became the official mouthpiece of Hungarian Nazis.

By the time the British Prime Minister, Mr. Chamberlain, hurried over to Munich in a desperate effort to appease the dictator, Father's candle of hope for a better world had long burned out. He was glued to the radio listening to the BBC as the Prime Minister returned to London after meeting Hitler. Stepping out of the airplane, Chamberlain held a document signed by both of them. He waved the paper high above his head for everyone to see and declared in a confident tone, "This is the guarantee for peace in our time." The moment he spoke those magic words the crowd around his plane broke out in wild jubilation.

But Father didn't. He sighed, and in a mournful voice I had never heard before said, "Poor Mr. Chamberlain. He's still as blind as I was two years ago." Father didn't want to hear any further news. He turned off the radio, picked up his pruning shears and went out to his beloved rose garden.

Listening to foreign broadcasts was not yet forbidden and those who knew the language listened avidly to French, English or German stations. The hotter the political tensions grew in Europe, the more time people spent huddling around the radio. Ours, a big box elegantly carved out of noble woods and with a dozen vacuum tubes glowing inside, was a masterpiece. The quality of the box, however, had no bearing on the quality of reception. It crackled, whistled, moaned and often didn't let out a whisper until banged on the head. You had to put your ear almost inside the box to get the long distance broadcasts the adults so eagerly wanted to hear. This had an unpleasant consequence for us youngsters: we had to remain quiet. Absolutely quiet. An unbearable strain when all we wanted to do was to run, jump, wrestle, argue with all the noise and energy of happy childhood.

It was Hitler's speeches I hated the most. They were so long and dull.

He usually started in a controlled voice using words of respect, understanding, and brotherly love. At times he even pulled God into his speeches. After half an hour he started to get excited, and by the second hour he was braying like a berserk donkey. For me, all he said was incomprehensible mumbo-jumbo, but the adults wouldn't miss a word. They wanted to know what that madman would do next.

There was, however, a sentence in one speech I fully understood and that I still remember today. He started in his usual style, and as he worked himself up to a crescendo he suddenly stopped for a moment, then continued with renewed vigor,

"Ab fünf Uhr fünf und vierzig wird zurückgeschossen."
"As of 5:45 this morning we are returning their fire." My parents looked at each other in stunned silence. They didn't have to tell us to be quiet; we understood without words. Their drawn faces told us something grave, something awful had happened. They sat motionless, lost in their thoughts. Finally one of them said, "This time he has gone too far. There will be war."

The date was Friday, September 1st, 1939. At dawn that day Hitler's army invaded Poland.

From then on, military actions developed so rapidly we could hardly follow them in our school atlas. Russia invaded Poland from the east and attacked Finland and the Baltic States. The Germans occupied Denmark and Norway and ran over Belgium, Holland and France at speeds never seen before. Europe was going up in flames.

Hitler and Stalin had signed a non-aggression pact the year before, yet Father Pataki, our history teacher, was worried, doubting their sincerity. "One day those two will get at each other's throats," he said. "Then God help us. We're between them; they'll trample us underfoot." This threat hung over our heads and everyone knew it, yet daily life went on as before. People quarreled, made love, complained about their neighbors or the price of potatoes, repaired leaking kitchen faucets and scolded children for muddying their shoes.

It was on June 22nd, 1941, that Father Pataki's prophecy became reality. Germany attacked the Soviet Union. We were awestruck by the speed with which Hitler's army advanced towards Moscow, but even more we prayed. We prayed for a deliverance from this evil, for a miracle to save us from the war.

Then on a clear, sunny morning, completely unexpected and unprovoked, a Soviet airplane bombed Kassa, a city in eastern Hungary. The plane flew low, the red star clearly visible on its wings and fuselage. It circled slowly over the undefended town and when it returned towards Russia, six people lay dead in its wake.

The uproar was enormous. The newspapers, fanning the fire of anger, carried pictures of the mutilated bodies on the front page. People demanded revenge. They wanted Hungary to join the war against the Bolsheviks. But others, more cautious, suspected a Nazi provocation.

"Do you believe this attack was planned by the Russians?" My brother, Jancsi, asked Father.

"Why would they do such a thing? The Red Army is retreating in chaos. Stalin is fighting for his life. He doesn't need additional enemies. He is cruel but not stupid."

"Could it have been a Russian pilot who lost his bearings and mistook Kassa for a German city?" Jancsi asked again.

"That's possible, but it's more likely the Germans had a

hand in this affair. They probably took a captured Soviet airplane, put one of their own pilots in the cockpit and sent him to bomb Kassa. They set a trap. I hope our government won't fall into it. We must remain neutral. We absolutely must avoid the war."

But Hungary didn't stay neutral. The next day, in an unwarranted hurry, the Prime Minister declared war on the Soviet Union. A few weeks later our army, and with it Jancsi, was on the front fighting the Russians.

What really happened on that early summer morning over Kassa, and who was responsible, remains a mystery to this day. There is no evidence to prove anything one way or the other and even history buffs gave up trying to solve the puzzle. The sad fact remains that Hungary was dragged into the war. But even without that provocation, who knows how long we could have stayed out of it.

Chapter 9

It's Getting Serious

Father Ambro put down the chalk, left the unfinished math problem on the blackboard and over the din of wailing air-raid sirens announced:

"Class is over, boys. We are going down. Don't run, don't shove and no talking. Just walk slowly to the ground-floor gymnasium. You know the routine. Join the other classes. The last one to leave opens the windows. We don't want them blown out. All right, move along."

Over a thousand of us squeezed into the hall, squirming, pushing and joking without a care in the world. A direct hit would have buried everyone alive with a single blow, but that was something only teachers worried about. For us these were fun times, especially when an alarm freed us from an exam. The anti-aircraft guns could be yapping like a bunch of mad dogs at the Allied bombers that flew onwards to blast Germany, but they didn't bother us. They created an awful racket with no damage as of yet. But on that sunny April morning of 1944, our carefree times ended.

The bombers came by the hundreds in close formation. From below, it looked as if a giant hand was slowly pulling a tightly woven carpet over the sky. This time they didn't just fly over harmlessly. They opened their ugly bellies and dropped all their cursed bombs on us.

As the bombs exploded all around, the only thing I still remember was the fear—that black, gripping fear that paralyzes you, and renders you unable even to scream. Today I wonder if the boys high above us in their flying machines were as frightened by our anti-aircraft guns as we were of their bombs. But on that day, I didn't see any trace of a human in those planes, only evil riding the gray, shimmering monsters, ready to murder us all and destroy everything we held dear.

Miraculously, our school escaped with only three huge craters around it—one between the school and the church, one next to the orphanage, and the third five meters deep in an empty lot. The minute the sirens sounded the all-clear sign, we ran out to gawk at the craters, laughing, joking, happy to be alive and pretending in the most perfectly macho way that not one of us had been the slightest bit scared, not for a moment.

"Hey, you guys," someone said, "don't be so cocky. If the pilot had twitched the trigger just a second earlier, none of us would be here anymore."

"Too bad for him—he should have stopped picking his nose sooner," was the reply. "Come on, let's play some soccer," and we ran over to the football field.

The next day, all schools in Budapest were shut down and remained closed until the war ended more than a year later. Parents sent their children to friends or relatives in villages. Since we had a cottage on Lake Balaton, Mother took us there along with the cook and maid. Only Father remained in the city.

In the villages everything was still at peace. Peasants plowed the fields with their teams of oxen, as their ancestors had done since time immemorial. Cows, dogs, pigs and goats knew nothing of the war. Food was plentiful so we didn't lack anything, at least for the time being. My friends and I biked in the hills, chased girls and swam or sailed on the lake, oblivious of dangers that still seemed so far away.

The nights were pitch black. If you didn't cover your windows with black curtains and a sliver of light escaped, the police would accuse you of sending secret messages to the enemy. Once or twice a week, however, the sky was lit up with what we jokingly called "Stalin candles." Dropped by Allied aircraft, these extremely powerful magnesium flares—bright as a hundred full moons—illuminated the entire countryside. The pilots could navigate by that light as easily as in daytime. Obviously they didn't need the glow of burning cigarettes to find their targets. Nevertheless it was strictly forbidden to smoke outdoors at night.

Occasionally we witnessed a daytime air show over the lake. The Allies had already conquered most of Italy and could send their bombers from there. But as they had too many aircraft for a single airport to handle, they had to take off from a number of airfields and used Lake Balaton, the biggest lake in central Europe, as an assembly point. From there they continued in a single roaring tidal wave to engulf yet another city. The Hungarian fighter-planes learned where to lie in wait for them, but the moment they attacked, American fighters appeared from high above to defend their fat bombers. As in a deadly ballet, the fighter-planes twisted and turned to the beat of blazing guns and screaming engines. They were shooting, smoking, burning, and occasionally crashing in balls of fire. Once, an American and a Hungarian plane fell in our neighborhood almost simultaneously. I zoomed over on my bike to investigate. In a desperate last minute effort, the Hungarian pilot had succeeded in ejecting from his burning craft, but his parachute hadn't opened. The American died still strapped in his seat.

With the passage of time, orders issued by the authorities became increasingly ludicrous. They warned us, for instance, not to pick up pencils supposedly dropped from above, as they could be filled with explosives. The Americans wanted to maim even children, they said.

Then around harvest time, when the wheat was standing high and dry, we were told the enemy planned to drop thousands of small firebombs during the night. These would ignite at the first rays of sunlight and turn all the fields into a blazing inferno. If the bakeries couldn't get any flour, the reasoning went, then soldiers would starve and the war would be lost. It was therefore our patriotic duty to stand watch in the night and squelch any bomb that could go off at dawn. Zebi and I were ordered to bicycle around the fields from three o'clock in the morning until the sun was high in the sky. Unfortunately, at this early hour the village dogs mistook us for ordinary thieves. I was more frightened of those vicious dogs biting my ankles than of being thrown into jail. So we deserted our sacred duty, and if the war was to be lost on account of it, well so be it. Those bloody dogs should have been kept on a leash.

By this time Adolph Hitler's great empire was crumbling faster than sandcastles on the beach. The Allies had landed in Normandy. Italy had surrendered and Mussolini was in captivity. Hitler himself had barely escaped an assassination attempt by his own generals and in his blind fury turned the screws of terror even tighter. In Hungary, the Russian army was advancing with irresistible force. Nevertheless the Nazi propaganda machine boasted incessantly of miracle weapons that would turn defeat into victory.

Of the flood of refugees who began streaming through the villages, however, no official ever said a word. People were fleeing the East, their horse carts piled high with chairs, tables, mattresses, sacks of potatoes, chickens, ducks and occasionally even a pig. On top of the pile, the very old were perched with the very young. Others trudged behind, pushing a loaded bicycle or a baby carriage, or pulling skinny cows towards the unknown. I couldn't watch this heart-breaking procession. Yet, like so many other things at that time, you would never have known this was happening unless you saw it with your own eyes.

Mr. Cohen could still keep his country store open. He

didn't let the yellow star on his coat lapel beat him down, but wore it almost as a medal of distinction. Some Jewish businessmen, however, had no illusions. They left all their possessions behind, took their wives and children and ran to a safe country while they still could. And although time was running out, Mr. Cohen decided to wait.

Mother often sent me to his shop to fetch sewing thread, a few pickles, a mousetrap or some other small item. It was dark in his store. The sole bulb dangling from the ceiling threw only a dim light over barrels of sauerkraut, jars of herbs or vanilla, boxes of nails, and bottles dripping kerosene. Only little Sarah brought color to this cavern as she dashed among the crates playing with her ever-present pink doll. Mr. Cohen, with black hat and curly side burns, would always sit behind the counter next to the window, dipping his pen into the inkwell as he entered each sale in the ledger.

"Here," he would say to me, "this is the change for your Mama, and here is a penny for you. Save your pennies, young man, and you will be rich one day." I found the old man amusing and never objected when Mother sent me on these errands, although fewer and fewer people dared to shop there.

At one peasant's house, a Polish military officer was hiding. A high school teacher in civilian life, he had escaped to Hungary when the Germans and the Russians invaded his country. All the local people knew his whereabouts, but nobody bothered him, not even the police. He gave us displaced city kids lessons in Latin and math, as getting to the nearest high school, 20 miles away, had become almost impossible.

Buses were plentiful, but fuel was short. Some clever engineer, however, had concocted a device that ran a motor on firewood instead of gasoline. Installed at the back of vehicles, these huge contraptions were fed with cords of wood, the fire meticulously adjusted and the smoke somehow pumped to the engine. Then, with luck and the help of all the saints in Heaven, the bus began crawling forward. But if your prayers were found wanting, then like a stubborn mule, it kicked off the apparatus, spraying hot ashes over all the passengers.

All this time the Russian front crept closer. Some people could hardly wait to be rid of the Nazis, but even more people detested the thought of Bolshevik rule. Then on October 15, 1944, as we prepared for Sunday dinner, the radio suddenly went still in the middle of a Verdi opera. The Head of State, the Regent Miklós Horthy, was to address the nation.

"We must accept defeat," he said. "It would be senseless bloodshed to carry on with the war. I have therefore ordered the Army to cease hostilities and begin negotiations with the Soviets for an honorable surrender."

We were stunned. After a long silence Zsuzsi sighed ever so softly: "Well, it's over. After four years this stupid war is finally over." Then she jumped up yelling "Hurrah!" and we all hopped into each other's arms hugging and kissing in pure joy.

We waited all afternoon, craving more details, but not a word came through the radio, only Beethoven symphonies played over and over again. After many hours we had enough of this interminable music. "Why doesn't the government say anything? Did something go wrong?" Father grumbled, chain-smoking as he paced the living room floor. Finally, an announcer we had never heard before came on the air:

"Regent Horthy has been arrested by German military forces. Mr. Ferenc Szálasi has been appointed Head of State. Under his leadership, the war against the Bolshevik enemy will be fought with renewed vigor. Opponents to the war and their Jewish masters will be liquidated."

"Oh, dear God," Mother cried, "why did you let this happen? That madman will kill us all." Her outburst sent shivers through me. In critical situations Mother's judgment was always right.

Many believed Miklós Horthy had been a mediocre statesman, but they also recognized that he had protected Jews and leftist sympathizers as much as he could without running the risk of outright German occupation. Jewish people had to wear the yellow star, but as long as Horthy was in charge, they were not deported and they could keep their property. Under him Hungary remained a relatively safe haven in the sea of Nazi terror.

Szálasi, on the other hand, was Hitler's worthy pupil. The venom of his speech was nothing short of his master's. His Hungarian Arrow Cross party was a mirror image of the German Nazi party, except for their emblem, which was a cross made of arrows instead of the swastika.

Now we knew we were in the last few months of the war, and that our survival would be a tightrope walk between Allied bombs, the German Gestapo and the Nazis among our own countrymen. Like earthworms after a summer rain, the first Arrow Cross members appeared with their party armbands minutes after the announcement.

Hardly had a week passed when, on the way to church, we met our neighbor from across the street, a man with whom we had a polite neighborly relationship. Already wearing his armband, he stepped in front of Father, looked at him with palpable hatred and stammered, "You bloody Jew-lover, watch out or we will wring your neck if you carry on what you are doing. We know you better than you think." Then he stepped aside and entered the church. I saw Father's jaw tighten, his lips narrow, but he remained silent.

There seemed to be no end to bad news. My Uncle Béla Johan, Mother's eldest brother, was arrested. But he enjoyed such high respect in the entire country that even the Nazis didn't dare eliminate him. Béla had graduated from medical school early in the century. He had spent a year in the U.S. on a Rockefeller scholarship, establishing good connections there. Later, when he became Secretary of State for Health of Hungary, these contacts proved to be very useful. Through his efforts our country received substantial sums of money from the Rockefeller Foundation for improving hygiene in the countryside. Thus my uncle had been able to install the first public health care system, have artesian wells dug for clean drinking water in every village, and build nursing stations to teach and help pregnant women and young mothers. Through all these actions, life expectancy in Hungary was dramatically improved. But by refusing Szálasi's order to dismiss Jewish doctors, he had committed a cardinal sin. He had to go. They deported him and his whole family to a remote village and kept them under house arrest.

A few days later the Polish officer didn't come to give us Latin classes. He had been taken away. We never learned his fate.

Chapter 10

At the Station

Things were changing fast now. Our village used to be a sleepy little place, where even the flies seemed to take a siesta at noontime. Loading cattle at the railway station was often the biggest excitement of the year. Once a big bull absolutely refused to be led into a boxcar. Three men pushed him from behind, and pulled him by his nose ring, swearing and cursing, but the beast simply refused to budge. In desperation a sweat-soaked, big, burly fellow grabbed a pitchfork and shoved it into the bull's behind, yelling "Move, you bugger!"

Well, the bull did move, but so did everyone else. First the three peasants flew into the wagon. Then the bull lowered his head and, with horns pointing towards the market, took on the village. Fruit stalls, goats, pigs, bicycles, everything took to the air. People screamed and ran for shelter and then the bull, with a pair of pants still hanging from his horns, demolished a horse cart. The horses reared up and, panic-stricken, took off with the remnants of the cart through vegetable gardens until they disappeared in a cloud of dust. In the end, man still triumphed over beast, but what a heroic fight that bull put up before it was led away!

Now young recruits were being loaded into these same

cattle cars and shipped to the Eastern front. Everyone in the neighborhood came to the station, throwing bouquets of flowers, kissing tearful good-byes, singing patriotic songs, waving handkerchiefs and praying that God would bring the soldiers back safely.

Then one day, as I passed by the railway yard, something was happening that I had never seen before. There was a small crowd on the platform—men, women and children, holding on to each other without a word. No one moved, no one spoke, the silence was absolute. Around them stood five or six policemen, bayonets glinting from the barrels of their rifles. They stood motionless, as silent as the others. The weather was balmy, yet the civilians wore warm overcoats and most of them clutched a small bag of clothing or a baby in their arms. Little Sarah Cohen was there, her pink doll pressed against her chest almost hiding a yellow star.

The crowd waited passively. Only one person in the entire station showed any sign of agitation. A skinny man was nervously walking up and down the tracks as if he could hardly wait for the train to arrive. He wore an armband with the arrow cross.

Finally a smoke-belching locomotive, dragging half a dozen cattle cars behind, stopped at the platform. One of the policemen flipped his hand, a sign for the people to embark. Two by two they climbed in, pushing small children up and dragging grandparents behind. They got on board in silence, not showing any emotion, as if they had been waiting for this day for a thousand years. Once a car was packed, the man with the armband closed and sealed the door from the outside and people started to climb into the next one. On her way Sarah dropped her doll. She tried to pick it up but someone dragged her away and she disappeared in the darkness of a wagon.

Slowly the station emptied of humans, and when the last car was filled and the train puffed away to its secret destination, only the man with the arrow cross remained. Arms folded on his chest he gazed contentedly after the train. He was the picture of a man who had done his duty and was proud of it. When he left, nothing but a broken pink doll remained on the platform.

I didn't understand what was happening. Why didn't they object, why didn't they scream, shout, kick? And why didn't a single man try to fight? I saw an old farmer standing a few hundred feet away, puffing on his pipe, seemingly deep in thought. He looked like a wise old owl, who could perhaps enlighten me. So I went over to him.

"Tell me, what's the meaning of all this? Where are they taking these Jews?"

He hemmed and hawed, played with his long, graying mustache, then hesitantly offered a few words.

"Well, I don't know, young man. I can only tell you what I heard from the barber's wife."

"What did she tell you?"

"Well, she said they're being taken to work somewhere, to make ammunition or to build air-raid shelters for the army. Something like that."

"Didn't she tell you anything else?" I pried further.

"Yeah, she thought it was good, because you can't make a soldier out of a Jew. They would run over to the enemy and become traitors. Can't leave them home either, she says, because they would just make more money, while our sons are killed by the Russians. I don't know if that's right, I'm just telling you what I heard."

"But why take the children?"

"Now, now, my young friend," he said with some irritation, "don't you have a spark of Christian decency in your heart? Do you think it would be right to tear children away from their parents, to break up families? No, it wouldn't. You must show some charity to these people, even if they are only Jews."

At that moment a woman, who had obviously been eavesdropping, interrupted our conversation.

"You two are talking a lot of nonsense. If you don't watch your tongues, you may end up in one of those cattle cars yourselves."

I thought that was good advice and took my leave from the old man. I still didn't understand what was happening, but I knew something was very wrong. I hadn't seen a single German soldier around the station, only Hungarians. The prisoners, the policemen, the man with the armband and the onlookers were all Hungarian.

Walking past Mr. Cohen's shop on my way home, I saw a man perched on a ladder blotting out the owner's name from the store sign. Having finished painting, the man climbed down and stepped back. Finding no more trace of Mr. Cohen's name, he wiped the sweat from his bald head and went inside. He sat himself behind the counter at the window, opened the ledger and began scribbling something. I was curious to see him close up, but I never did. Mother stopped sending me there.

Chapter 11

Victor

A week or so later my good friend Victor telephoned. "Hey, Gyuri," he said, "I'm in your neighborhood. I'd like to see you. Can I stay with you a couple of days?"

"Sure, buddy, the sooner you get here the better."

I knew we would have a good time for Victor and I had been friends since time immemorial. We started elementary school together; we played wild games and created a lot of mischief, and as we got older, we had many a good discussion about God and the Universe. He also had a cute sister who was my partner in dance school and his mother used to bake the most delicious cookies for the parties at their place. Politics never entered into our friendship, although his father was an important figure in the Arrow Cross Party, a real staunch Nazi.

When he arrived, we fooled around, made a lot of racket, punching each other as a sign of great affection. I was really happy to see him and was somewhat taken aback when Mother pulled me aside and whispered to me the moment Victor was out of earshot.

"Be careful what you say to him Gyuri, you know who his father is."

I promised to watch out, but I didn't worry much. After all, I was always open with Victor.

We spent the day hiking and biking in the Bakony mountains, enjoying all that life could offer. Exhausted by late afternoon, we lay down under an apple tree, stuffed ourselves full of fallen fruit and speculated about the forbidden world of sex. All in all, we had a wonderful day.

When we awoke early next morning, Victor suggested that we go frog hunting.

"Listen Gyuri," he said, "I brought along my air gun. We could go down to the swamp and bump off a few of those fat croakers. It should be real fun."

"I think that's a lousy idea Victor," I replied. "Why should killing frogs be such a great fun? They are harmless. If you want to hunt, then let's go after mice. They do a lot of damage."

But he insisted on frog hunting and I tagged along. Victor was a good shot and seldom missed his target. He must have finished off a dozen when he wounded a particularly large male and watched intently as the animal slowly, painfully, wiggled to death.

"That's how they should blast those fat Jews," he yelled. "Let the vermin wiggle before they die."

'Jesus,' I thought, 'what bit this guy?' It took me a few moments before I could face him.

"Tell me Victor, if I had a yellow star sewn to my sweater, would you want to shoot me, like you shot that frog?"

He came closer, poked the barrel of his gun at my chest and laughed.

"But Gyuri, you are not a Jew. Relax my friend."

I didn't know what to say. Hateful talk about the Jews was nothing new. I had gotten used to it. The radio, the newspapers, and the Arrow Cross people talked like that constantly. But this was my good friend Victor. Suddenly I was scared of this fellow who a minute ago had been my trusted buddy. I felt as if the earth had opened up and in one ugly bite swallowed ten years of friendship.

Mother's warning was suddenly very clear in my mind. I closed up and kept my mouth shut. Victor hadn't noticed that anything had been painfully and irreparably broken, for as he left he thanked my mother profusely for our hospitality, repeating over and over again what a wonderful time he had had. When the door closed behind him Mother gave a great sigh of relief.

I never saw him again. I heard some forty years later that a day before the final collapse of the Nazi system, he and his father managed to escape to neutral Portugal together with a bunch of high ranking party members. In their great hurry they had left his mother and sister behind to fend for themselves.

Among the boys I used to hang out with at school, Ferenc Corin was different. Like a few other chaps in the class he was Jewish, but he was also rich. Not just wealthy, but fabulously rich, though he never flaunted it. His family owned the biggest manufacturing company in Hungary. They smelted steel, made motorcycles, tractors, knitting needles, aircraft engines—you name it, they made it. Suddenly Ferenc and his entire large family disappeared.

As we found out years later, he was not taken to Auschwitz in a cattle car like poor Mr. Cohen, but was flown to Switzerland by the German SS in a disguised military plane. When they landed in Zurich and the entire extended family of forty-one arrived safe and sound, a large sum of money was transferred into a numbered Swiss bank account. I don't recall the exact amount that was told to me, but it seemed more than a king's ransom.

Chapter 12

Before the Siege

By early December 1944, the front was ominously approaching. One morning I went with Father towards the East to see what was happening. Once we got close enough to hear the roar of the battle, we scurried back to the house.

Father, usually a man of quick decisions, couldn't make up his mind whether the family should stay at the cottage or go back to Budapest. He was talking more to himself than to me when he said, "The neighbors are all gone. It's not good to be the only man with three women. I can't do a thing if Russian soldiers want to take them. In the city it would be easier to hide them."

"Well, then, why don't we go?" I asked. He lit a cigarette and continued, looking even more worried.

"You know, a house-to-house battle in Budapest could be vicious, and our home on the hill is very exposed to artillery fire. At City Hall they offered me a safer building for the time of the siege, but I haven't seen the place. And the food? Where would we get food in the city? I don't know what we should do."

When we got back, he admitted to Mother that he couldn't make up his mind. "Your intuition is good," he said. "You decide."

"We go back to Budapest," Mother replied without a trace of hesitation.

Father let out the biggest sigh of relief I ever heard escape him, his eyes perked up and he became his active self again. "Let's pack right away," he ordered. "We'll leave at sunset. The planes can't shoot us in darkness."

Five adults, two children and my baby nephew had to fit in a car the size of a Volkswagen. All essentials were tied down to the roof: a barrel of sausages, bags of dried beans and flour, the smoked hindquarter of a pig and assorted suitcases. What couldn't be piled on top stayed behind. The spare jerry can of gasoline was too valuable to carry on the roof. A desperate man could cut the rope and disappear with our spare fuel. Getting stuck on the road without gas, with the enemy on our tail, was too frightening to contemplate. So we took the fuel can inside and I sat on it.

The moment the sun dipped below the horizon we crowded into the car and hit the road. As our home disappeared behind us, my sister, Vica, remarked, "It's so strange to leave the house wide open with all our stuff still in it."

"That way at least looters won't have to smash the doors," Father replied as he carefully squeezed the car onto the highway between two oxcarts. Trucks, cows, bicycles, pedestrians, tanks and soldiers all mingled into one huge fleeing chaos. There was no passing or stopping. A horse went mad and was shot. A car had a flat tire and was shoved into the ditch by a tank, its passengers forced to proceed on foot.

That was a very long night, full of fear, discomfort and unfulfilled needs. We couldn't even stop for a pee. Finally by sunrise we reached Budapest and drove straight to the house the authorities had assigned to us. It was a neat-looking one-family home, but squeezed in between two six-story apartment blocks, it would be vulnerable not only to a direct hit, but also to the collapse of the neighboring buildings.

The house was uninhabited, the air stale, and the furniture

covered with a thin film of dust. I opened a closet and found it full of clothes and children's toys. There was an unfinished meal on the kitchen counter and spiders had already spun a web on the arms of the Menorah.

"This is an eerie place," Vica said. "The people are gone, but their spirit is still living here." Suddenly it became clear to whom the house belonged. "They were deported," Father said. "We can't take over their home. We will not stay here. We're leaving."

By this time it was getting late. The children were cranky, the baby had had no warm milk all day and we still had no place to stay. We were getting pretty desperate when Csöpi, my sister-in-law, suggested we go to her parent's place only a few blocks away. Their apartment was spacious enough for two people, but to squeeze in our entire family as well would be a challenge. Yet her parents were so happy to have Csöpi and their grandson under their roof that they took us all in.

So we piled in, all eight of us, plus the smoked hindquarter of the pig. It was tighter than tight, but we thought we could hold out for a couple of weeks.

Chapter 13

The Siege

By the sixth year of the war our airforce still had a few fighter planes left, but their fuel tanks were empty so they couldn't fly. Pilots could only watch helplessly from the ground as waves of enemy planes bombed Hungary with almost complete impunity. Yet Father, like a magician pulling rabbits out of a hat, had always managed to conjure up a jerry can of gasoline to keep his car going. His was one of the last to run in Budapest, until one day a man wearing an arrow cross armband tore up his license and took the car at gun-point.

From our fifth-floor apartment bordering on the ghetto we could see how Jews from all over the city had been herded together. The streets leading to the ghetto were then sealed tight with brick walls. How people got food, how they managed to survive, we had no idea. Still, compared to their brethren in towns and villages they were lucky. By the time their turn came to be shipped to the camps, trains couldn't run anymore. Locomotives, tracks and bridges lay in ruins, forcing the Nazis to leave many of these people behind. Thus many survived.

Early in the month, my brother, Jancsi, arrived from the front for a furlough. Father tried his best to keep him home, pleading with him to stay.

"The war is nearly over, just a few more weeks," he argued. "Please don't go back. Dress as a civilian, we'll hide you. I can forge you some documents. I've been doing it for Jews; I'll do it for you. Think of your son and wife. Please don't throw away your life."

We knew he was pleading in vain when Jancsi replied:

"You're right, this war is senseless. But I'm an officer. Men are entrusted to me. I can't abandon them while they face the enemy. I gave my oath as officer. I will keep it. You know how much I'd love to stay home with my baby. But, Father, I must do my duty."

Mother didn't engage in the discussion. She seemed to feel the weight of that impossible choice between Soviet bullets on the front and a firing squad at home. At this point she had put all her hope and trust in God's hands.

For Mother was fighting a battle of her own. She was desperately trying to save my eight-year-old diabetic brother, Tamás. She analyzed his urine, drew blood samples three times a day, measured every gram of hydrocarbon he ate and calculated the insulin she had to inject before each meal. Later, in the makeshift air-raid shelter down below the apartment block, squeezed in among sixty strangers in the cold, damp, candle-lit darkness, she would struggle for his survival. But slowly she was losing the battle. Tamás would fall into coma, screaming and convulsing more and more often. Father managed to buy insulin on the black market, but that didn't seem to help anymore either.

To add to my parents' worries about their eldest and youngest sons, suddenly my future became a problem, too. On the 10th of December, the army ordered all sixteen year olds into battle. As the situation turned hopeless on the front, the leaders became desperate to delay the day of reckoning. Just to gain a few weeks, they were willing to sacrifice all and everyone. In Hungary we were still lucky, for they had not conscripted boys younger than sixteen. But in Germany, Hitler had gone completely berserk. He was sending kids thirteen years old to the killing fields. The youngest I met was only nine when a rifle was thrust into his hands. There were no uniforms small enough to fit those children, so they had to wear armbands to identify themselves as soldiers.

Father would have none of this. He forged a birth certificate making me a year younger, and sent me away to work in a textile factory in Kőbánya, an industrial suburb where no one knew my true age except my sister, Zsuzsi, and her husband Feri, the manager. I had mixed feelings about this. On the one hand I was glad to avoid the army, but on the other I was petrified every time youngsters came with their armbands and submachine guns to check for deserters. Had Father's work not stood up to scrutiny, they would have put me to the wall without hesitation, for child-soldiers were at times more brutal and fearless than regular conscripts.

The last days of December were strange. To the West, Budapest was still open, but to the East the Russians were only a mile away. The Red Army that had advanced with such great speed towards the city suddenly stopped and didn't move for six weeks. Not a shot was fired on either side. It was eerie.

We knew we could be run over and life could end any minute, yet bureaucrats kept on shuffling their papers with zeal and our machines continued spinning and weaving colorful fabric. In the carpentry shop, I sanded and polished wood to perfection and got hell from the foreman if the job was not done just right. At the same time, water reservoirs the size of swimming pools were dug all over town in preparation for the day when the pumping stations would fail. White arrows were painted onto buildings pointing to the shelters so that rescuers could more easily find buried victims of an air raid. Then one day red onions disappeared from the market. People had bought them all up, believing these would protect them from typhoid. At home, Zsuzsi was cooking and baking for the Christmas celebrations, toys were bought, diapers changed, games played. But the stillness was strange, like living on a volcano about to erupt any moment. We just waited.

On Christmas Eve, after the presents were distributed and we were about to sit down for dinner, the telephone rang. It was Feri's sister calling from the western end of the city. Instead of the expected season's greetings, she spoke only a few nervous words.

"The Germans are gone. The Russians have arrived. They're OK. We're not hurt, but hide your watches—they stole all of ours. Didn't even look for weapons, just watches," and she hung up. We tried to call back half an hour later, but by then the telephone lines were cut.

Feri admired the cunning of the Russian generals. Good chess players, they had known when to make their move. They had waited patiently for Christmas Eve, when the German soldiers sat down for a little celebration and even relaxed with a drink or two. At exactly eight o'clock, they struck with lightning speed. The surprise was so overwhelming that hardly a shot was fired as they sealed off the only opening left around Budapest, closing the trap door on 100,000 soldiers and a million civilians. Now slowly they would pull the noose tighter until the city was strangulated.

The telephone call from Feri's sister relieved some of our worst fears. Herr Goebbels, the Nazi propaganda minister, was a liar after all. The Russians didn't have horns, nor did they eat newborn babies for breakfast. We finished dinner and let the children enjoy their new toys for a while before kissing them good-night. The adults played a game of Mahjong, then Zsuzsi slit open the belly of a doll and sewed in all our watches. At midnight we turned in to wait and maybe sleep.

In one desperate move, the German army tried to break out towards the west, but failed, and Hitler would not allow them to surrender. The stage was set for a house-to-house, inch-by-inch battle. Like two years earlier at Stalingrad, the siege of Budapest had begun.

It was around noon a few days later when there was a knock on the front door. Four German soldiers stood there asking politely if they could warm themselves up a bit. We let them in. Zsuzsi offered slices of her Christmas cake and even brewed up cups of ersatz coffee, she felt such a pity for the poor boys. Three of them were younger than I. Only the sergeant was a bit older, perhaps seventeen. With their spotless uniforms, polished boots and well-oiled guns, they could not yet have seen much battle. The conversation soon came to the subject occupying all our minds.

"You know the war is nearly over. It's lost. It's finished," said Feri, a courageous statement he would not have dared utter only a week before. But now with death breathing down our necks from so close, we didn't give a damn about the Gestapo or its Hungarian clone, the Arrow Cross henchmen.

"Yes, we know," answered the sergeant dolefully. There was no sign of the crisp *Heil Hitler* anymore. No trace of hope for the miracle weapons either. Just deep, bottomless sadness.

"Well, then, why do you carry on fighting? Why don't you surrender?"

The sergeant chose not to reply but one of the young ones piped up proudly.

"A German soldier does not surrender. I will die for the honor of my Fatherland."

There was nothing more to say. They thanked us for the hospitality, picked up their guns and left with a polite *"Auf Wiedersehen."* We knew the Germans would fight to the bitter end, but when and how that last battle would take place no one could predict.

On New Year's Day, the family got out of bed a little later than usual. Zsuzsi's children, still in pyjamas, fumbled with their toothbrushes as we reckoned with another day of interminable waiting. The grandfather clock standing in the hall had just chimed nine when the volcano erupted. But this was not just a regular volcano—it was Hell itself blowing its top. Thousands of artillery pieces opened fire at the same moment along the entire front. The Russians must have been shooting everything they had, all at once. The Devil himself must have lent them fire. It was too dangerous to run across the yard to the air-raid shelter, so we just pushed the children under a bed, piled all the cushions on top of them and crouched under the door posts. We also prayed like never before.

After fifteen minutes, just as abruptly as it had started, the shooting stopped. We were unhurt. The Russians were aiming at the front line a mile away, but even from that distance the noise almost drove me crazy with fear. I never understood how anyone survived up there, let alone kept on fighting. Still the Germans did.

The artillery barrage over, Zsuzsi ran to the air-raid shelter with the children. Feri, his brother Jozska, who was a priest, and I stayed behind to throw shirts, dresses, suits, towels, blankets, bed sheets and everything within our reach into a heap on the floor. We poured water over the pile, opened the windows to the freezing air, and scurried after the rest of the family. Zsuzsi had thought of this clever plan—no one would be able to take a thing out of that ice block till the spring thaw, neither us nor looters.

Our shelter was nothing more than a glorified cellar room ten feet below ground with steel doors over the openings. An emergency water tank stood in one corner and folding cots for about fifty people lined the walls. It was not much of a refuge, yet to be deep in the dark womb of mother earth felt comforting. With a plank and two wooden boxes, Jozska even managed to set up a makeshift altar where he celebrated holy mass every morning. But since there was no toilet in the shelter, we had to run upstairs at the risk of our lives. "Blessed are the constipated," people murmured.

For some of us youngsters, curiosity was simply irrepressible.

We just had to see what was happening outside. One day a fellow rushed back all excited. "A horse was shot—the poor thing is still kicking." Men immediately grabbed knives and axes to finish off the suffering beast, returning a few minutes later with big chunks of delicious meat.

At three o'clock on January 4th, 1945, the lookout entered the shelter with a solemn face, as if he could hardly believe what he had witnessed. "They're gone. The Germans are gone." There was dead silence. We looked at one another but no one spoke. Even eyes were silent from behind the blank expressions. So this was it. A hateful era had ended and the new one had not yet begun. For a while we hung suspended in no-man's-land.

Slowly people rose off the bunks and shuffled to the middle of the room. Mothers picked up their babies, pressing them to their breasts. Fathers took little children by the hand and stood with their families. We waited in this soundless limbo for what seemed an eternity, maybe five minutes. Then suddenly the clatter of running boots broke the silence. Fifty pairs of hands shot up in the air at once.

"Nemetsky, Nemetsky!" shouted the soldiers, swinging their guns at us from the door.

"Nyet Nemetsky, Vengersky!" 'No Germans, only Hungarians,' replied a man who spoke a few words of Russian.

"Kharosho. Davay chasy, davay, davay." 'OK, let's have your watches.' They dashed around picking off the watches still left on raised arms.

In less than a minute they were gone, leaving us standing bewildered. So that's how history is made, I thought. Then from the back someone barked a crude cheer. "Fuck Hitler, long live Stalin." Yes, a page in history had indeed been turned.

The war had finally rolled over us. We still heard its thunder and felt the tremor of distant bombs, but by next morning the front was already a few hundred yards further to the west. Curious to explore the leftovers of the battle, I slipped out of the shelter moments after the last bullet had whizzed by.

To my surprise, our house was still standing amid the rubble. Half of its roof was gone and torn trees blocked the entrance, but it looked livable. A burnt-out tank smoldered in the courtyard surrounded by heaps of discarded weapons and ammunition. There were hardly any people outside the shelter, but near the garden fence I noticed a couple of kids poking at something with a stick.

They were gawking at the German soldier boy who had come to our kitchen to warm himself a few days earlier, the boy ready to die for the honor of his Fatherland. Well, he did. Did he save its honor? Was he a hero to his beloved country or just a brainwashed fool? Did it really matter? He was dead.

Sure, I had seen dead people before, but grandmother Nanóka hadn't really been dead. She had just lain down for a rest, her head on a fluffy cushion, white hair nicely combed, eyes closed, rosary in her folded hands. She was sleeping peacefully. Smiling in her dream she might have been listening to the songs of angels, a music so beautiful she decided never to return.

But this boy wasn't sleeping in peace. Arms and legs spread out on the muddy snow, a trickle of blood frozen at the side of his gaping mouth, steel helmet off, hands still clutching the rifle, he couldn't have heard angels sing over the roar of cannons. It was his bulging blue eyes that sent a shiver through me. Death itself was grinning at me through those eyes. It snickered, licked the blood from frozen lips and jeered, "I'll get you too, my little friend, sooner than you think," reaching for me with icy claws. I turned to run, but stopped when I saw the white skin of the soldier's feet. They were bare. Someone had robbed him of socks and boots while the body was still warm.

I wanted to scream and curse. "You bloody vultures,

you hyenas! Don't you know when to stop? Kill and get killed—that's OK, that's war. But you can't rob the dead. That's cruel! It's forbidden, disgusting! What if I were lying there? Would you rob me, too? Would you hyenas tear socks and shoes off my feet as well? You would, you bloody bastards, wouldn't you?"

I was fuming. It took time to calm my anger. I rummaged a long time among the ruins before I could see that vulture for what he was: just a poor bastard needing boots more than the dead. I left the memory of that thief in God's care, relieved that I still had boots on my feet. The children stayed behind, playing with the soldier's shiny medals.

A few days later a light snow was falling as I went out scavenging. Abandoned, the corpse was still there, but mercifully the snow had covered his piercing eyes. He couldn't have noticed when I removed his rifle.

It's better I take it, otherwise it may fall into the wrong hands, I reasoned. And who knew, it might come in handy one day. I kept it hidden in the attic until much later, when the new government created a police force and started executing people in possession of a weapon. Then I packed it, well-greased, into a wooden crate and buried it together with a pile of ammunition under a lone tree in a vacant field.

More than a week passed before the cadaver was carted away in a horse-drawn buggy. It had frozen to the ground and had to be pried free with a pickax. Only German corpses were on the cart. The victors had already buried their own dead, draped in flags, to the sound of bugles. Civilians got buried fast as well, but without music. I thought of the mother of that soldier boy searching for her lost son. When would she finally give up hope? Would his father miss him, or was he lying somewhere under snow as well? My thoughts flew to my brother, Jancsi. Where was he, and did he have his boots on?

Chapter 14

After the Siege

For a couple of weeks chaos reigned supreme. The Government, the police and everyone of the old Nazi regime had disappeared, leaving behind a power vacuum. Angry crowds broke into jails to liberate political prisoners, letting thieves, robbers and all the assorted riff-raff escape in the confusion. The Soviet generals' top priority was to win the war, not to worry about law and order in the conquered territories. Soldiers occupying the land behind the front line could loot and rape with impunity.

Women tried a thousand tricks to turn themselves into old witches—smearing ashes, garlic powder or rancid grease over their hair and clothes. But try as they might, young women couldn't metamorphose into grandmothers nearing the safe age of ninety. They hid in coal sheds, attics or under beds. One woman practiced vomiting by pushing her finger down her throat—she believed nothing would cool a soldier's desire quicker than throwing up on his frisky little tool at the crucial moment.

My friend Egon's forty-three year-old mother ran out of luck one day as she went out to get food for her family. Three soldiers ambushed her on the street and gang-raped her in broad daylight. She didn't resist—for that would only have extended her agony, nor did she scream—as they would surely have knocked her out. Later, after her torture, she philosophized calmly, "That's war for you. Men are killed. Women are raped. I only hope I didn't catch some disease." And she proceeded to prepare supper for her children.

Booze was as irresistible to the Russian soldiers as were women. After they had emptied all the wine cellars and breweries, they guzzled down the alcohol of drugstores and the perfume found in beauty parlors. When that supply was exhausted, some of them went after the alcohol in the sample jars of medical schools. It was rumored that a few went blind from drinking that stuff.

Soon after the arrival of the Soviet Army, a couple of soldiers took Feri to the factory office, where an army captain was already sitting in the manager's chair. The officer was explaining something in Russian, of which Feri didn't understand a word. But from his forceful body language, my worried brother-in-law understood the Captain would take the factory for the Red Army and the manager's house for his own use. He would let us stay in the underground shelter.

The officer marched over to take possession of the residence. Zsuzsi was there with her three young daughters, trying to clean up the mess of broken windows and fallen plaster. Later, she described the encounter.

"I heard steps coming. I looked up and saw the officer and a soldier heading for us. I wanted to run, to hide. But when the Captain saw us, he stopped. We looked each other in the eye. I was ready to tear his out if he touched my children. Then he turned towards the girls. For a while he stood motionless, open-mouthed, just gazing at them. Then he squatted down to their level and caressed their hair while talking to them in the softest, gentlest voice. He pulled out his wallet and showed the picture of his young wife sitting on a bench surrounded by three small girls. He pointed at his daughters and named them one by one. They were blond just like my children, and the same age as well. Then he kissed the photo and put it back in his pocket."

After that, the Captain didn't want to take the house anymore. Half the living room would be plenty for his needs, he said. He even helped push cupboards around and hang a few blankets to divide the room. Finally he pointed to the soldier standing at the door, "That's Ivan. He will guard the house."

This was fantastic. We would be safe in the house from looters, robbers and rapists. The Captain even kept Feri as plant manager.

With time we learned a few words of Russian and he a bit of Hungarian so we could have rudimentary conversations. Occasionally we also shared a meal together. Sometime soon thereafter, two young female soldiers moved in with the Captain and we saw considerably less of him, while the noise coming from the far side of the blanket wall intensified substantially.

"Mami," asked little Marika, "why are the ladies crying so much? Is he hurting them?"

"No, darling, they are just having fun. Lots of fun."

Ivan also could become very emotional about his wife and children. Every time he looked a bit too deeply into the bottle, his eyes began watering, and he would pull out a wrinkled photo from his pocket to kiss his wife and son frolicking on the shores of the Volga. But a minute later he would grumble about the Captain having two female soldiers and he none. "Why can't he pass me at least one of them?" and he would mutter a litany of swear words while taking another long sip of whatever was in his bottle.

By early evening Ivan could seldom stand guard anymore. We used to put a cushion under his head and pull his rifle aside so that he wouldn't hurt himself on his bayonet. He could sleep and dream, yet this snoring symbol of authority was enough to keep intruders from our door.

What went on during the first few months of occupation had different names. We called it looting, the Russians justified it as war reparations. When we took something from them, we considered it repossessing our own property, but they saw it as stealing and got very mad about it. So call it what you will, everybody played the game. But one day I went too far, risking not only my life, but also the family's well-being. I was stupidly reckless.

The factory had gradually been put back into operation, mostly weaving cloth for the military, rather boring stuff. But one day a truck arrived with exquisite, colorful silk thread, so soft that only older workers remembered ever having touched such material. The most skilful of them was to weave it into cloth fit for a queen. Apparently it was meant for the mistress of Marshal Malinovsky, the supreme commander of the Soviet Army in Hungary.

On a Sunday afternoon when the factory was closed and only watchmen and the families of managers were allowed to be in the courtyard, I ambled around the buildings with Judy, the accountant's daughter. She was seventeen and a very gutsy Jewish girl who had survived the holocaust by luck and cunning. I was telling her how tempted I was by the idea of repossessing the silk cloth.

"Well, go for it. Take it. It belongs to us. I'll stay outside and keep an eye out for watchmen," she offered.

I couldn't resist the combined temptation of silk and Judy. The lock on the gate was old and easy to pick. Inside, with all the machines quiet and no steam whistling through the pipes, I got scared in the eerie silence and hesitated. But then I grabbed my pocketknife and with a few quick moves slit the cloth off the machine. I pulled off my shirt and pants, wrapped the material around my body and put my clothes back on. In a minute I was out of there. I locked the gate and waddled back to the house like a fat duck. I even listened to a few of Ivan's jokes before going up to the attic to hide my loot.

Monday morning when they noticed the damage, the Russians exploded. Their reaction was way beyond what I had expected. "I'll find the saboteur" roared the Captain. "I'll kill the bastard with my own hands. I'll shoot him before they court-martial me. Imagine stealing the Marshal's silk! Oh, you bloody bastard, just wait."

He carried on raving and shouting. He threatened to kick Feri out, ordered all 1,200 workers to be frisked through and through, and called for the help of the military police. While the Captain was stirring up a tornado, even Ivan seemed frightened and stayed away from his bottle and stood ramrod straight all day. The entire plant was turned upside down, but luckily nobody thought of searching the attic only six feet above the Captain's bed.

But like all storms, this one also blew itself out with time and I traded the silk for a motorbike.

Chapter 15

My Brother Tamás

One sunny spring day, I went to the front yard to pick up discarded ammunition that began to appear through the snow with the first crocuses of the season.

In the far distance, I could still hear an occasional explosion reverberate from the city center. I hated that sound. Father, Mother and my two little brothers still lived there. Or did they? We hadn't heard from them for five weeks. I had already collected half a wheelbarrow full of hand grenades and bazookas when I suddenly noticed a man on crutches hobbling towards me. He had a plaster cast on his right leg, soaked through with dried blood. He was a pitiful sight altogether.

"Is this where the Balázs-Waigand family lives?" He asked as he reached me, and when I nodded he said, "I bring news from your parents."

I didn't dare ask what the news was; I just kept staring at his wounded leg. As he noticed this, he looked around to see if anyone was within earshot and whispered:

"Ah, don't worry about my leg. There's nothing wrong with it. I put the cast on to fool the Russian patrols. They have the habit of dragging able-bodied men off to work. They have no use for cripples, so I decided to hump along on these old crutches. But could we go inside? I have important messages for your family."

Once the entire household was assembled around the kitchen table, he gave us the news we were so much hoping for.

"Your parents are fine. And so are Eva, Péter, and your sister-in-law and her little baby. They are fine. Nobody got wounded. The house they are living in was damaged, but it's still standing. They were lucky they didn't get a direct hit."

We were elated by the good news. In our excitement none of us noticed he had omitted Tamás' name. Zsuzsi served the man a bowl of potato soup and yellow corn bread. He ate slowly, stopping once or twice as if to say something more. Finally he pushed away the unfinished food, looked at me and then at Zsuzsi, and blurted out:

"Your little brother Tamás died from his diabetes two weeks ago." At first we couldn't comprehend what he had said. During the siege people were killed, shot or crushed under collapsed buildings, but nobody died of illness at such a time. We sat in silence. After a while the man quietly carried on:

"During the last days of battle Tamás fell into a coma in the air-raid shelter. Your parents took him to what remained of the hospital, just a basement where the wounded were crowded together. A doctor diagnosed appendicitis and operated on Tamás by the light of a kerosene lamp. The appendix was not inflamed. The operation had been unnecessary. Tamás died the next day in a diabetic coma."

My sister began sobbing quietly as the man continued.

"Your parents wrapped him in bed sheets and pulled him to the cemetery on a borrowed sleigh. There was no priest, no funeral service, only your parents saying prayers over the makeshift grave." Then the man expressed his sympathy and left. He had messages to deliver to other people, he said.

In the silence that now surrounded us, pictures from the past emerged before my eyes. I had loved to play and fool around with my two smaller brothers. I made them march and salute like soldiers, row my boat like galley slaves. We climbed the cherry trees and stuffed ourselves with the ripening fruit till our bellies couldn't hold anymore. But everything had changed when Tamás was diagnosed with diabetes.

I wanted to play on as before, but was often scolded for not being gentle with Tamás. Our games became more subdued. As the months went by and his condition worsened, my parents devoted more and more time to his care. I sensed their despair, but I couldn't understand it. Father even gave up smoking in the hope his sacrifice would appease God and heal his little son. It seemed Mother lived only for my brother's healing and had no more time for me. It was as if Tamás had stolen her from the rest of us.

I became jealous of him and grew angry with my mother. I think I even began to hate Tamás. When he fell into one of his comas, convulsing and trashing, I was frightened that he might die. Yet I longed to regain the attention of my mother.

Now it was over. It was too late to play, to be angry, to hate, even too late to ask for forgiveness. I was lost in a whirlwind of feelings. I rose from my chair and, leaving Zsuzsi crying and hugging her children, I went out to clear the rubble from the front yard and the turbulence in my heart.

This picture of the Johan family and my father was taken around the time of my parents' engagement in 1914. Standing (left to right) Béla, Victor, Mária, my mother, Pál Balázs, my father, and Hugo. Sitting: Nagymami and Nagypapa

Mária Johan

"Mother, judging by her early pictures, was an attractive young woman. From her soft, gentle smile and almost dreamy look in these photos, one would never guess the enormous strength of character and quiet wisdom that, combined with kindness, were the hallmarks of her personality."

Pál Balázs

"An early photograph of my father as a naval officer in the Austro-Hungarian Navy shows a tall, strongly built man with black hair and eyes that look straight into yours—the confident picture of a handsome young man with a strong personality and determination."

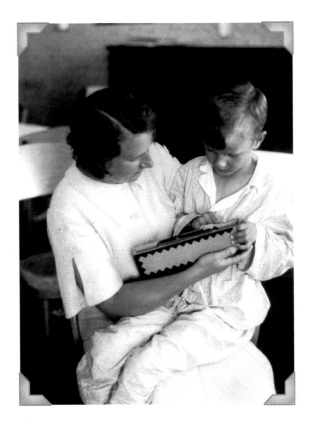

The toy, my mother's parting gift, before I was left in the sanatorium of Stolzalpe for nine lonely months in 1935.

Who was I offering flowers to? My memory does not carry me that far. As a passionate photographer my mother caught many such moments of our early childhood.

I started sailing at an early age on Lake Balaton, but even at twelve I still had trouble with hand-me-down bed sheets as sails.

I'm the big brother here, with Tamás beside me and Péter next to him. Mari, Zsuzsi's first daughter, was Tamás' age and shared in many of our games.

My brother Tamás was perhaps the handsomest of us all. He's about four on this 1940 photograph.

A rare picture of all the Balázs siblings together taken in the early forties. The differences in age were such that a few were already adults when the youngest was born. From right to left are Zsuzsi, Jancsi, Éva (Vica), Gyuri (me), Péter and Tamás.

This is one of the cars that came out of my father's short-lived automobile factory in 1935. While Henry Ford was making cars that looked like black shoe boxes on wheels, Father's automobiles had fahionable design and colors. Too bad this venture bankrupted him.

Chapter 16

The War is Over

In the middle of February 1945, after six long weeks of house-to-house battle, the guns had finally gone silent in every corner of Budapest. The Nazis were history. There was no more reason for me to hide my true age in fear of military conscription. I tore up the false birth certificate Father had fabricated for me and moved back to the small apartment in the city center where my parents were cooped up with two other families.

That winter had been bitterly cold. People could have frozen in their windowless apartments had they not stayed in cellars huddled with neighbors for a little body heat. But the cold had one advantage, which was that the dead could be collected and buried before they began to decay. For now that the shooting was over, what we feared the most was the outbreak of a typhoid epidemic. How many soldiers and civilians lost their lives in the city we will never know since nobody bothered to keep a tally. Some estimates went as high as 150,000 dead, or more than 3,000 a day for the forty-two days of the siege.

When retreating, the Germans had blown up the seven bridges over the Danube, and now twisted steel reached out of the water like the arms of drowning men. Electricity, gas and running water were just a memory. We had to fetch drinking water in buckets from the municipal swimming pools. Hardly anything moved on the streets, only Soviet tanks which rambled over the ruins like giant cockroaches.

But even after a volcanic eruption, sooner or later a blade of grass will appear and life will start blooming more vibrant than ever. So it was in Budapest. On the first warm spring day, people mushroomed out of the cellars and music filled the air: Gershwin, Glen Miller, Louis Armstrong, and all their tunes that had been forbidden during the Nazis times.

One April evening the light bulb hanging in the kitchen flickered for a moment as if awakening from hibernation, and soon there was light. The following week the faucets started to cough up an ugly, brown goo, but after a while water gushed out clean and clear.

Even Mr. Grossman, our old neighbor, came home from the ghetto. Pale, haggard and shrunken, he staggered up the five flights of stairs, grabbing the iron railing with one hand and holding his pants up over his emaciated body with the other. He looked around as if seeing his apartment for the first time and whispered almost apologetically, "I'm back. They had no time left to finish us all off. But my Rebecca, she will not come back anymore," and he disappeared in the empty darkness of his home.

It was the 6th of May, if I remember well, and we had just finished our usual meal of beans, when Father suddenly pricked up his ears and said, "Quiet please. Listen to the radio." And then we heard it. Hitler was dead. Germany had capitulated. The news electrified Father. He grabbed his chair, put it on the living room table and, armed with a kitchen knife, climbed on top. He reached for the huge smoked ham hanging from what was once the crystal chandelier's hook, and with a quick swipe of the knife cut down the beast. "No need to save this pig for emergencies anymore," he cheered. "Let's celebrate." And did we ever!

By June the Cistercian monks managed to reopen our high school. Since streetcars and buses were still not running,

Péter and I had to walk two hours every day to get to school, making a long detour over an emergency pontoon bridge crossing the Danube.

It was great to be back at school and to find most of our friends again, but learning became incidental. There was just too much going on for us to pay attention to the teachers. We turned the place into a flea-market, bartering stuff we had scavenged from the ruins—car tires, tools, shoes, guns, sticks of dynamite, everything imaginable. I was good at this business and ended up owning a motorcycle. The best, however, was the delicious warm food, full of meat and noodles that the Swedish Red Cross dished out to students every noon.

On the way to school we had to pass by the Astoria Hotel, which the Americans had fixed up as the seat of their High Commission. The building had no more bullet holes, there was glass in the windows and the frames were painted gleaming white. I can still see those window frames, the only white in the sea of gray that was Budapest.

There was always a crowd milling around observing the rosy-cheeked Americans walking in front of the Commission in spotless uniforms. They chewed gum, drank Coke and munched on hot-dogs—things we had never even heard of. And they had cigarettes, the currency which now replaced worthless banknotes.

"Look at that guy," a woman said, "he's smoking like a chimney. They must be Lucky Strikes or Camels. What I wouldn't do for a pack of cigarettes."

"I know what you'd do, you'd jump into bed with him," snickered a young man.

"Damn right I would and so would you, you little bugger." And they kept on bantering and dreaming.

By this time it was safe to walk the streets during daylight hours, even for women. But in the evening it was advisable to carry a gun or else you could get stripped. Thugs would hold you up and take your clothes, socks and shoes, leaving you stranded in your underpants.

One day during the first week of August news came that the Americans had dropped an enormous bomb on Hiroshima, forcing the Japanese to surrender. It had something to do with atoms, they said. We jubilated. Finally the war was really over, no more killings anywhere. There was peace on the planet. But Old Mr. Grossman just sighed.

"Too bad they didn't drop that thing on the Nazis four years ago. They would have saved a lot of trouble for the world."

Chapter 17

Shattered Hope

A year had passed since the end of the war and life began to flow peacefully. Order gradually reappeared; there was no more danger of being robbed, mugged or raped, and people started to rebuild their lives. We could now safely leave our relatives' tiny downtown apartment where we had squeezed in with two other families. The musty, jam-packed flat had been a relatively secure refuge during the battle, but now we felt we were suffocating. The poor toilet had to work overtime, and whenever it got plugged pandemonium broke out. After a year it was definitely time to move on.

But where should we go? Our home on Mount Gellert had been hit by several artillery shells and had become unlivable. However, just a few blocks from it, on Balogh Tihamér Street, stood an empty building with only its roof and windows blown away. The owner had fled to Switzerland and would let us use the house if we did the renovations. With the few gold coins Father had hidden away at the outbreak of the war he could afford a new roof, but glass couldn't be bought, even with gold. So we simply glued paper over the windows, smeared it with cooking oil to make it translucent and weather-resistant, and settled in.

Convinced our future would be bright and happy after so many years of tribulations, we felt every day was better than the one before. The only grave concern remaining was the whereabouts of my brother, Jancsi. Since his departure for the Eastern front two years before, we had had no news of him. He was missing. We prayed and waited and never gave up hope. And then, on a glorious summer day in 1947, even this cloud lifted as Jancsi stepped through our door.

He could hardly walk, he was so frail. He told us that prisoners of war had received extra food rations a fortnight before being shipped home from Siberia. In spite of this, he looked like a scarecrow. As we hung on his every word, he gradually recounted stories of life and death in the camps.

"Once on a long march during the winter I couldn't go on any further and collapsed in the snow. I wanted to die. A guard kicked me, but I didn't budge and he left me for dead. I don't know how long I lay there when the image of Csaba suddenly appeared in front of my eyes. An irresistible urge grabbed me: I had to see him, I had to cuddle my little son again. That picture gave me the courage to get up and drag myself all the way to the camp. That's how I survived that day and many others that followed. But not all did. At night when the fleas left a neighbor and came over to you, you knew that poor chap had given up his soul."

Jancsi learned to knit in the camp, converting worn out sweaters into socks and mitts. Since he was very skilled with his hands, the guards would often bring him things to repair.

"This way I kept my mind occupied," he said, "and I also earned an extra ladleful of soup or a slice of bread. Being busy helped to keep my sanity and my will to live."

Slowly Jancsi regained his strength and got a job, and we all enjoyed the good things that began coming our way. We even had an election, just like in the West, with political parties, free speeches and all the trimmings of a democratic society. After all, when they had met at Yalta, Stalin had promised Roosevelt free elections would be held in Eastern Europe.

This was real exciting stuff—the younger generation had never experienced the heady atmosphere of a real political campaign. Maybe the old ones didn't remember one either. At night Jancsi and I worked for the Small Landholders Party. We zoomed around on my motorcycle holding buckets of glue on our laps, brushes in our hands ready to paste every flat surface with our posters. If we saw a Communist placard, splash, we slapped on our own banner. Five minutes later another party's slogan covered ours. By dawn the glue and paper was all spent and it took us hours to scrub the sticky stuff off our pants, socks and hair, but it was worth it. Holding fast to that gummy brush made me feel I was carrying the torch of liberty in my hands.

Our party won a resounding victory, somewhere around 50% of the votes. The Social Democrats came in second place, while the Communist Party collected a measly 12%. Thus Stalin had fulfilled his bargain with the American president; he did allow a democratic election. But the old fox had never said a word about what would happen after the ballots were counted.

He allowed the formation of a Hungarian government, but only if it was a coalition of all parties, the Communists included. This was a disappointment and the first sign of trouble to come. Yet it had to be accepted since a great number of Soviet troops were stationed in our country. We were naïve enough to believe that perhaps a junior portfolio like the Ministry of Sports would satisfy the demands of our occupiers. But we were badly mistaken, for the Russians now insisted that the Communist Party control the Ministry of Interior, the department that in turn controlled the secret police.

This was a cruel awakening. The terror of the German Gestapo had hardly vanished and already a new monster, the Soviet NKVD, had descended upon us. Our hopes were shattered. Our dreams were turning into nightmares.

It didn't take long before we felt the noose tightening

around our own family. As manager of a textile mill, Father had his hands full rebuilding the company from the ravages of war. He liked to tell us about the progress they were making. One evening he was talking with great enthusiasm about the fact that finally all his machines were repaired, when he suddenly stopped in mid-sentence.

A police car had come to a halt in front of the house. We froze at the sound of approaching boots. The steps got louder and louder until they stopped at our entrance. For a moment there was dead silence and then the dreaded knock on the door. Three secret-service men burst in and took Father away.

Mother took us by the hand. "Come children," she said, "we have to pray for Father." We lit a candle under the statue of the Virgin, fell on our knees and prayed as hard as we could. At dawn Father was back. "The walk home took many hours," he said, "but the grilling at police headquarters was very short. I am fired." Then he told us what had happened.

"Comrade Balázs," the interrogating officer had asked, "are you prepared to resign from your job? And will you do so of your own free will?" After a long pause the policeman continued. "I am sure you will, once you think about the alternative. But you know, unfortunately we can't pay you any compensation or pension. After all, quitting is your idea, isn't it?"

Father tried to think but the officer spoke again.

"Well, Comrade, make up your mind—or do I have to convince you further?" and he dropped his rubber truncheon on the desk with an ominous thud. A gorilla of a secret-service man, who had been lounging in the corner of the room, suddenly stiffened up and moved closer, cracking the joints of his massive fists.

Father understood, took the pen the officer proffered, and signed the pre-written document. The officer stamped the paper and said, "You grasp things fast, Comrade Balázs. You are a very smart man. You may go now."

The morning papers brought the news that my father had resigned for health reasons and a new director, a party functionary, had been appointed to replace him.

A few weeks later, Father, the indestructible optimist, joined a man who was in the business of stitching flower decorations onto kerchiefs. Their clever little hand-cranked machine stitched fifty at a time and Jancsi was appointed chief crank-turner. But it wasn't long before the authorities got wind of this capitalist enterprise and closed it down like all private businesses.

Without any income, our money was running out fast. Had Jancsi not hit upon a clever idea we would have gone hungry. He began weaving carpets out of rags on a loom he had built. We all pitched in to help. Péter and I did some weaving after we got home from school, Father bought the rags and found buyers for the finished carpets and Jancsi's wife, Csöpi, dyed them in bright colors while Mother cooked and kept house. Our family enterprise was enough to put some food on the table, but not much more. Nevertheless this venture was also doomed to fail. Soon the Government nationalized the rag business and from then on only state enterprises were permitted to collect rags. That was the end of it. No rags, no riches.

I also tried to bring money into the family kitty, but with different methods. My motto was, if the government robs us of everything, then it's fair game to steal from them in return. My technically-inclined school friend, László, had taught me how to doctor gas and electric meters so that they registered only a small portion of the consumption. Once I had mastered all the tricks, I went to fix utility meters most evenings. My clients were so happy for the savings that they paid me generously. Besides the money, the best thing about this illegal undertaking was the sweet sense of revenge in cheating the Government out of something.

Gradually the Communist Party took control of every aspect of our lives. They nationalized everything: factories, houses, apartments, bank accounts, cars, cottages—anything of value. It became foolish even to decorate your home, since that might tickle the fancy of a party hack, who would have you deported to a one-room shack in a dusty village with nothing more than the clothes on your back. Many of us kept a small bag packed with a toothbrush and our most precious personal belongings near our beds, in case there was a knock on the door in the middle of the night.

But our government had no monopoly on confiscating people's property. The Soviet Army was also great at liberating us from our earthly belongings.

One day I was riding my bicycle in shorts and a T-shirt on a deserted street, stupidly wearing my watch visibly on my wrist. This was just too much temptation for a Russian soldier who appeared out of nowhere and decided that from now on he would ride my bike and that he needed the watch more than I did. I was furious, but even more so when, talking to my father about this adventure, he asked, "Why did you let him have it?"

"But Father, he had the gun, and I didn't even have a stick."

"Even then, use your brain. You're smart enough. Don't let yourself be pushed around by anybody."

I didn't understand his outburst. Did he want me to risk my life for a lousy watch and a rusty bicycle? Or was he still angry at himself for not putting up a fight when the Secret Service robbed him of his job?

To soothe my anger, I decided to steal back from the Russians as much as I could. Close to our home was an army depot full of truck tires, batteries, barrels of oil, boxes of grease and jerry cans of gasoline. That became my nightly hunting ground. The fact that it was heavily guarded made the danger even more enthralling. Crouching under a truck while the boots of guards pass only inches from your nose is a fantastic thrill. I must have confiscated from the Soviet army ten times the value of what the soldier had stolen from me.

I had made a particularly good haul one night, when Father broached the subject of my dangerous business. "All right, you've proven your point. Don't you think you should quit while the going is good?"

I knew he was right. My luck couldn't have held out much longer. Now fully satisfied with my exploits, I stopped these excursions. Instead I devoted all my energies to studying, and none too soon. With all the excitement, my high school performance had nose-dived. I hadn't failed any exams, but no one was admitted to university with only minimal passing grades. My life's dream of becoming an engineer could vanish if I didn't get down to business. I had only four months until the all-important final senior matriculation exams, so I began studying ferociously, determined to succeed. To my great relief, I graduated with honors and was admitted to the Technical University.

"That, my boy, was a last-minute awakening. Congratulations on your success," beamed my proud father.

Father had few things to be happy about those days. He was a very energetic, enterprising man who had managed to pick himself up every time he fell flat on his face. He had had a couple of enormous business crashes in his life, but he shook off failures like a wet dog throws off water. This time, however, he felt he could not fight the system. Every time he got back on his feet, the Communists pulled the rug from under him. It was just too much.

An eternal optimist, he had believed we could always build a better tomorrow if we just tried a bit harder. But now the road didn't lead to greener pastures. The Stalinists pushed the country deeper and deeper into a bottomless pit. He was losing hope.

He was also a deeply religious man who believed that whatever happened in life ultimately happened for a good reason, even if we couldn't see its purpose at the time. He accepted the death of my little brother Tamás in all humility as the will of God. But what was happening in the country now was not the work of the Lord but the machinations of Evil. He seemed to lose even his faith.

Hopeless adversity left its mark on him. The man who could laugh so heartily became morose, withdrawn. My once-energetic father now sat at his desk for hours, playing cards, alone, day after day. He had never had a long fuse and now it was even shorter, lashing out in anger at the smallest irritation.

I now believe he went into a depression, although at that time the word was unknown. Mother protected him, but I didn't understand his suffering. As a teenager, I found the chaos swirling around us exciting, full of a million wild things to do. He, now over sixty, saw his world in ruins, more thoroughly destroyed than our once-proud city.

Slowly we drifted apart. In my teens I avoided him and his critical outbursts. After a while we had nothing to say to one and other. I was angry and sad at the same time. I loved my father but loathed what he had become. I started thinking of leaving home to go away, far away, beyond the sea.

With time he overcame his depression. He got a government job as packaging expert and gradually regained his self-confidence. Energetic again, he wrote a textbook on packaging and returned to his eternal hobby, gardening. Not content with simply planting and pruning bushes and trees, he even wrote and illustrated a book entitled *The Evergreens of Our Garden.* By then I had left Hungary, but I was happy and proud that even Stalin's henchmen couldn't break my father's back.

Seven years passed before I could see my father again. In 1956 he was sent to Italy on a short research mission. I flew over from Canada and we were able to enjoy three wonderful days together—two grown men respecting and loving each other. On the third day, the party delegate who had been shadowing us all the time cut short their visit, taking Father back to Hungary. As his train faded away in the distance, I sensed I would never see my father again.

Chapter 18

A Day in Worker's Paradise

For a couple of months during the summer of 1948 we exchanged our places at the Technical University for a workbench in a factory. I was lucky, since I was sent to the Ganz Diesel Motor Company, the most famous of all engineering works in Hungary. There I would learn much more, I thought, than in a smoky, sweaty steel mill, where many of my classmates had to go. I was full of expectations when I entered the factory the first time.

My learning curve was steep, particularly the first day. After filling in all my papers and getting my pass, I was led through the shop. We threaded our way carefully among the dilapidated wooden crates filled to the brim with shiny parts, spilling their excess onto the greasy floor. The lathes and milling machines were lined up in a row in front of the windows. The glass must have survived the war, for no machine smoke could have deposited so much soot as to be impenetrable to light in just three years. Leather belts from one long crooked shaft drove the machinery, the leather squeaking as if it wanted to go back to the cow from which it came.

Miska, the machinist who was to be my instructor, was in his mid-thirties, a likeable, good-natured fellow. He looked somewhat scraggy, his fingers dark brown, more from nicotine than from the grease and soot that covered everything. He seemed happy to have an apprentice, since this allowed him to goof off even more than was the custom in the shop. He was an old-timer and knew the ropes. His instructions were brief but to the point:

"Now look here Comrade Gyuri, with this lever you start and stop the bloody machine. The crank here pushes the grinding wheel to the work piece and this here is the control gauge. You must grind the part so accurately that it fits the gauge. It's easy; you can do it. By the way, these ship engines we're building are for our socialist brother, the great Soviet Union. War reparation payment, they say. They expect us to outperform the quota. The Party wants to be proud of us. Did you get all that?"

"I guess so, Comrade Miska."

"Well, then get to work, Comrade. Build socialism, but watch your bloody fingers. Don't let this lousy machine cut them off for you."

The instruction thus terminated, my conscientious teacher left me for the toilet. The poor fellow must have had the most awful constipation because an hour passed and he was still nowhere to be seen. In desperation I pulled levers, turned cranks and produced great amounts of sparks, smoke and noise, but very few parts to satisfy the gauge. The scrap box was filling rapidly. I looked desperately to the other machinists for help, but all I got was nodding heads and benevolent smiles. My God, I thought, they must know the punishment meted out to saboteurs, nobody even wants to be seen near me.

I was nervous when Miska finally returned with a happy grin after having accomplished his important task. I was afraid he would kill me when he saw the bulging scrap box and the near-empty product container. He noticed my utter distress, then looked at the two boxes for a long moment and said in disbelief,

"Holy Mother of God, you sure screwed up quite a big pile of parts, my little friend."

"I'm sorry, Miska," I mumbled in fright. "What should I do now?"

There was a long moment of silence as he savored my misery before uttering the absolution,

"Don't shit in your pants, Gyurikám. We don't live in the capitalist world anymore. This is Workers' Paradise. That's where we are now. You're a worker. No boss would dare to give you trouble anymore for a little mistake like this."

"I get that, but what about war reparations for the Soviets? They will think I am a saboteur."

"To hell with them! The Russians are a bunch of goddamn thieves! They stole enough from us to make up twice for any damage we did to them during the war. Let them paddle their bloody boats up the Volga without our engines."

Perplexed after this unexpected turn of events, I steered the conversation to safer ground and inquired about the art of grinding valve stems to the required tolerance. We worked like that the rest of the day—that is, Miska worked and puffed on his cigarette, while I watched him in restless silence.

When the whistle blew, we were already at the gate with our hands and faces washed, dressed in our city clothes. I said good-bye to Miska, and as I walked towards the street-car stop I wondered how long it would be before they took him from Workers' Paradise into police custody. I hoped that would never happen. I liked him.

Chapter 19

Encounter with the Army

We had a very good summer in 1949. It was warm but not too hot. A perfect time to kayak down the Danube with friends, and camp on the islands where nothing intruded on the silence but the croaking of frogs.

That summer could have been superb indeed, but for the threat of military service hanging over our heads. Everyone over twenty was being drafted by the Communist Army, but who wanted to waste three years of his life trudging through muddy training fields while obscenities were shouted at him by an egomaniac sergeant? Unfortunately, dispensation from service was rare, granted only in case of serious illness.

My buddies and I spent many hours discussing how we might simulate some disability when our time to muster arrived. The challenge was to turn ourselves momentarily into invalids and then regain full health once the doctor declared us unfit to bear arms. None of us could think of a good way of simulating a nasty disease, so we had to fall back on manipulating our heartbeat.

"One liter of strong coffee and a dozen aspirin will do the trick," suggested one.

"You'd better make it real black coffee. This ersatz stuff

we drink won't do much for you. And throw in two dozen aspirin if you really want to have the shakes," said another.

We searched through the medical encyclopedia for several evenings, but sadly we had to conclude that our only defence against the Communist Army was strong coffee and a few tablets of aspirin.

The prospect of frittering away years of my life in the army was a strong incentive to do something drastic. Emigration became an interesting, although dangerous, alternative. Dangerous, since there was no way of leaving a socialist country but to escape. If caught at the border, I would be beaten black and blue by the police and locked up for six to twelve months. This I considered a risk well worth taking! On the other hand, if I tried to skip the country as an enlisted man, I would be deemed a deserter, and the army didn't fool around with deserters!

These ruminations came to an abrupt halt when the mailman delivered the dreaded command. I was to report for muster at the city barracks the next morning. I went as ordered, with no defence but my trusted good fortune. As I arrived at the barracks, I realized the building was actually quite nice from the outside. A three-story yellow brick edifice in the baroque style, with big windows from the ground level to the roof, it had been erected at a time when Emperor Franz Joseph had peace in his Empire and spare money for such frivolities. Its location right in the center of Budapest, on the corner of the two busiest streets, may not have been very strategic against an invading enemy, but it was ideal for keeping His Majesty's unruly Hungarian subjects calm.

It would have been nice to philosophize away the day, but eventually I had to go in, strip down stark naked, line up with a hundred-odd similarly naked young men and slowly shuffle forward to the examination hall on the ground floor. The window facing the street was wide open, letting in plenty of light but not enough air to dissipate the heat and smell of all those nervous bodies. The doctor, sitting in front of the window, scrutinized the recruits with a bored look and then pronounced their fate with equal detachment. From the sidewalk, the good citizens observed the proceedings with noticeable glee.

The medical routine was always the same. After a quick glance at the throat, ears, nose and eyes, the order came:

"Lift up your penis with the left hand, take a deep breath and cough."

"Now turn around and bend over."

And finally the dreaded words:

"Fit for service. Next."

The crowd on the street was enjoying the show, judging by the giggling of the women when a particularly robust fellow had to hold up his family jewels. At least somebody is appreciating this degrading business, I thought, but why this forced exhibitionism? Getting fresh air into the crowded room wasn't the reason, as there would have been easy ways to screen out the view. It seemed the real purpose must be military training! Young men must be humiliated, ridiculed, subordinated, their self-respect destroyed, their individualities crushed, so as to transform them into simple morons, capable of blindly executing any order.

Suddenly there was noise and commotion in front of me. A big, strong fellow, sweating and shaking, had just finished the examination and before the doctor could give his verdict, he dared to talk:

"Sir, Doctor Comrade, may I respectfully request a heart examination, I believe I have..." but the poor guy couldn't finish his sentence before the doctor exploded out of his lethargy.

"You bloody bastard, you cheating son of a bitch! You think I'm completely stupid? You think I don't know what games you bastards are playing? A bit too much coffee and aspirin, eh? You take me for an idiot? Well, I'll fix your problem! Not only are you fit, but fit for the toughest jobs. Next."

I stepped forward, cursing that guy for making the doctor raving mad. I knew now that all hope had vanished. Nobody had been rejected yet that day. I stood there motionless for what seemed an eternity. The doctor gazed through me into the distance as if I were not even there. Slowly the deep purple vanished from his face and after a minute of silence, one could almost see a shimmer of kindness in his eye.

"My dear boy," he said softly, almost whispering, "you are very, very skinny, far too skinny to serve in the army. Go back to your mother and ask her to fatten you up a bit. We might call you next year. In the meantime, good luck, and God bless you," he sighed in a hushed tone only I could hear. Then he raised his commanding voice, "Next."

What had happened to me? Why this miracle? I saluted smartly, found my pants where I had left them half an hour before and ran out into the street with a new lease on life.

Passing the open window, I couldn't help joining the giggling girls. I stopped, not to peep at the naked men, but to search the face of the doctor. He was sitting in front of the window with the same bored expression as before, giving orders and calling out with the same detachment, "Fit for service. Next." What could have gone through the mind of this middle-aged man during that brief moment of angry outburst? Was his fury truly directed against that poor boy or aimed at the system, the Communist system, that was humiliating him as well and was in the process of destroying his humanity? During that short, silent moment when I stood in front of him, perhaps he remembered that he had once known kindness and love. Did he want to prove to himself that he still had some?

I was happy for myself, but saddened by the dismal future awaiting my buddies. Luckily, by the time I got home, Mother had a big pot of steaming goulash soup on the table, just as the doctor had ordered. We chatted as we ate and my gloomy thoughts began to evaporate. But I knew my turn would also come if I stayed much longer in Hungary.

Chapter 20

The Decision to Leave

Even today I sometimes ask myself what was so unbearable in Hungary to make me leave my country. By the end of 1949, this was a dangerous undertaking. There was no way of emigrating legally, and trying to sneak through the Iron Curtain meant risking jail at best or a bullet at worst. Still I decided to escape.

I didn't reason. I didn't analyze. I simply followed my heart. I left because my intuition told me to. But isn't this the way we always make the big decisions of our lives?

There were, of course, a number of things I wasn't happy with, perhaps none of them important enough to push me out of my home and country, but together they became an irresistible force.

One thing I was sure of, I loathed the political situation. The Communists were tightening the noose around our necks more and more. Life had become increasingly dismal. If you spoke your mind, you could expect the dreaded knock on the door in the middle of the night. That life wasn't for me. I wanted to be free.

There were so-called free elections. Everyone had to go and vote. You could cast your ballot for the Communist Party or against it. That was your only choice. When I went to vote, a scrutineer handed me my ballot with a smile and said, "If you wish to vote for the Party just fold the paper and slip it into this box. No need to mark it." Surprised by this blatant directive, I stared at her. Slowly her smile changed into a frown. "But if you are against our Party," she continued, "you must put a cross on the ballot." For a moment I hesitated, then marked the paper with a big cross and dropped it into the box. Visibly annoyed, she took a pencil and did the same to my name on a list. In the evening the radio announced the Communist Party had won over 98% of the votes.

In this way I was amassing black marks at an alarming rate, but the most damaging was one I collected during the Mindszenty affair. Cardinal Mindszenty, a very courageous man, was known to have resisted Hitler and now he did the same to Stalin. He was the most admired man in the country and therefore he had to be silenced. The police tortured him and dragged him before a kangaroo court. But the government wanted to create the impression that this was happening by popular demand. At the university they herded us into the largest auditorium, handed a petition for his execution to a student in the front row and expected each of us to sign it and pass it on.

Slowly, row by row, in absolute silence the document made its way around. The party hawks were watching from the side. Occasionally a fellow just passed it on without signing where his name was printed. That's what I did. My friend, Jano, who was sitting beside me didn't sign either.

On top of it all, there was the threat of military service hanging over my head. To waste three years of my life serving in the Communist Army was just too much to contemplate.

A totally different issue, which may seem trivial in light of the political repression, but nevertheless was very important to me, was my relationship to my father. Like many boys of my age, I rebelled. He was a strong-willed man, for whom children's education could only be achieved through strict control. I felt he would crush me if I stayed under his roof much longer. Mother told me, "Your Father loves you very much. He is strict only because he wants the best for you." Yet I couldn't feel his warmth, only his high expectations, which I was seldom able to fulfill. I felt controlled and yearned for more breathing space.

Then there was Emmy, my first love. She was seventeen. We had met, and that was it—we fell into that crazy, marvelous ecstasy you can only know when you are very young and have never been kissed. I had believed our bliss would last forever, but as she began dreaming of kitchen utensils and talking more and more about the color of our future bathroom towels, my ardor slowly cooled. And when her mother mentioned the word "wedding," I flew into a panic. I had to run fast and far away before they trapped me into holy matrimony. At that moment the other shore of the Atlantic barely seemed a safe distance.

At twenty, my wanderlust surely played an important role as well. I wanted to experience something new, to see what was on the other side of the hills. I was restless.

I clearly remember the moment when Jano and I finally decided to escape Hungary. It was a hot August day and we were climbing up to the ruined palace of King Mathias, high in the forested hills of Visegrad. We sat down on the broken walls of that six-centuries-old fort, dangling our feet over the valley and enjoying the quiet beauty of the place. Far below, the Danube made a ninety-degree turn towards the south and the distant Black Sea.

"Isn't this a beautiful sight," Jano remarked.

"It sure is the most beautiful sight in Hungary," I agreed. "But look, on the other side of the Danube you can already see Czechoslovakia."

"Yep, and beyond that somewhere is Austria, and beyond that France, the Atlantic and finally America. It must be exciting to see all that."

"Why don't we go then? What are we waiting for?"

"And to hell with border guards and their bullets?" he said.

"Yep. To hell with them. And to hell with Stalin and all the Communist bastards."

For a moment he looked at me completely mesmerized. Then he burst out laughing, raised his arms in a victory salute, shouting, "Look out world! Here we come!"

Chapter 21

Escape

My parents accompanied me to the end of our street to say a last good-bye. Our hugs and kisses must have looked casual, even happy, to any neighbors who might have taken notice of us. If people ever became suspicious of what I was up to on that September morning in 1949, Mother would have to pretend I was leaving for a university in faraway Miskolc. I knew how hard it would be for her to lie, but it would be essential for their own safety.

A week before, when supper was finished and I was alone with my parents, I had announced my decision to escape Hungary. For a long while Mother sat dumbfounded, her hand aimlessly sweeping a few breadcrumbs back and forth on the tablecloth. Then she spoke slowly, with long pauses between each sentence.

"I had hoped this day would never come, but if you must leave, I'll let you go. I understand you, but I'm scared for you. Gyurikám, where will you go? To which country? What will you live on? How will you finish university?"

I took her hand without a word. I had no answers to her questions. Yet deep down in my heart I knew somehow I would succeed. At twenty I felt invincible.

When Father spoke he was very calm, but couldn't hide the turmoil my decision created in him. Together we weighed the risks of my escape against staying at home. Remaining in Hungary wasn't without danger for me, but there were imminent dangers on the frontier as well.

"You can't go directly towards Austria. The border is sealed tight," he said. "Anyone trying to go that way is either shot or blown to pieces on the minefields."

"I know, Father, that's why Jano and I want to go the long way around to Czechoslovakia and from there to Austria. Apparently the Czechs haven't laid all the mines yet. We must pass before they do."

Finally Father took me in his arms and said, "I wish I could give you some advice, my son, but I can't. Whatever you decide, we will accept and live with."

And so on that Sunday morning, as we stood on a street corner, awkwardly parting, our hearts were filled with fear and pain. I don't remember saying anything. What can you say to your parents when you are possibly seeing them for the last time—"Don't worry, I'll be all right"? Or some other platitude? Maybe I did say that, I don't know. When I left them, I couldn't look back. I just walked towards the railway terminal.

Jano was waiting for me at the station. We chatted noisily like two young men heading to the hills for a pleasant weekend hike. As the train started to move, we jumped on board and began our long journey to unknown destinations.

I felt elated by the coming adventure. At the same time, I was scared of the dangers ahead. As the familiar landscape swished past the window, I inwardly said good-bye to the people, the fields and forests I had known all my life, when suddenly a firm voice yanked me back to reality.

"Your tickets, please."

The man wore a conductor's faded blue uniform, threadbare at the knees and elbows, and greasy at the neck, but it was a uniform nevertheless. I was nervous. We had learned over the years to beware of men in uniforms, even if the color of their outfit changed—gray, blue, brown or green, with brown shirts or black, swastikas and iron crosses or red stars, hammers and sickles on their shoulder pads. We had seen them all. And they never meant anything but grief to us.

"So, you're going all the way to Miskolc, one way, eh?"

"Yes, Comrade, going to finish my studies there, stay for a year," I lied with ease.

"Not a very nice place, still a lot of ruins left from the war. Only ten miles from the Russian border."

I didn't reply, just thanked him as he punched my ticket. Did he want to pull me into a conversation? Was he just a decent fellow looking for some distraction, or would he have denounced me had I said a wrong word? It was best not to take a chance.

After an hour's ride north of Budapest, a mile or two from the Czech frontier, we got off the train. The little village, whose name I have long forgotten, was like dozens of others scattered over the Great Plains of Hungary. Being Sunday, the church was packed full, like all the churches during the Communist rule. Some went to pray, but just as many went as a political act, to show defiance. Praying to God was the only sign of dissidence the Party still tolerated.

In the dense crowd, I could hardly kneel down at communion and Jano had difficulty reaching the confessional. In the eyes of the congregation, he must have been a great sinner for he spent an unusually long time confessing his trespasses. Little did they suspect he wasn't there for spiritual guidance but for something much more down-to-earth. He had gone in search of a guide to lead us to the Czech border. The confessional was a safe place to talk and the priest inside was a distant cousin of his. We hoped he might know a reliable person to take us to the border. When my friend finally stepped out with the radiant face of a repentant sinner, I knew we had our man.

Once the mass had ended, we mingled with the village folk outside the church, then drifted over to the back entrance of the presbytery. Within the tall stone walls, the garden evoked a feeling of peace and security. Wooden chairs and a long table stood under a centuries-old linden tree. We sat there and waited for the twilight hours. Our priest came out once to bring us food and explain to us the arrangement with the guide. The man, who remained nameless, would come while there was still some light and would lead us to the Ipoly, a shallow little river separating the two countries. We were to pay half the money when he arrived and the other half at the river shore. The sum amounted to slightly more than a worker's monthly salary. Not bad for a half-hour's walk in the fields, but very little if he got caught and had to spend a year in jail with us.

Guides were usually cunning young peasants, familiar with the routine of the guards. If they were caught, the police had ways of softening them up and turning them into informers. From then on, they would direct the fugitives straight into police traps. Apart from our trust in the priest, there was no way of knowing if we had a guide or an informer.

The sun crept very slowly over the sky that afternoon and there was plenty of time to talk, plan and browse through the poetry books the priest had lent us. Our long wait in the presbytery finally ended when the garden gate opened and a man in his late twenties approached us cautiously. He didn't shake hands or greet us as we silently surveyed each other. He had a muscular body, deep brown eyes and an open, friendly face that I thought I could trust. When he asked, "Are you ready?" I had no hesitation in slipping a wad of bank notes into his hand and saying, "Let's go."

First we walked leisurely through the village, stopping here and there as he pointed out a particularly rich fruit tree, or explained the merits of different milk cows. To others our casual little stroll must have looked innocent, just a couple of ignorant city folks admiring the beauty of country life.

His instructions, however, became more to the point once we reached the empty fields.

"Beside that haystack over there, there is an open gully. It runs down to the Ipoly. This time of the year there is hardly any water in it. When we reach the haystack, lie down in the ditch and disappear. I will slowly walk forward while you crawl along in the ditch beside me. If I should see soldiers I'll walk away from you to distract them. In that case you just stay low and wait. I'll come back for you when it's safe."

We did exactly as told. He was right, there was no water in the ditch, but it was filled with all the creepy, crawly, slimy creatures the good Lord had ever created. Progress was slow and disgusting as we moved along on our hands and knees. Meanwhile, our guide presented the perfect image of a conscientious farmer surveying his crop of sugar beets. He walked slowly, occasionally kicking a lump of dry earth, then bending over, pulling up a beet and inspecting it closely.

We had been slithering on our bellies for maybe half an hour when he spoke again. "You are now fifty feet from the Ipoly. There are dense bushes on the shore. Hide in there and wait till midnight. Then cross the river. But keep quiet and keep your eyes open. Good luck!"

He bent down as if to pull up a beet. I slipped another wad of bills into his hand and the next moment our nameless guide had vanished in the gathering darkness. We could sit up in the bushes, stretch and swat the mosquitoes feeding on our dirty faces. What a relief! But soon a new doubt started buzzing in my head. Was our guide straight or had he been turned informer already? Why did he tell us to wait? Wait for what? The soldiers? Was this a trap? We thought army boots were approaching every time a frog jumped. Shouldn't we cross right away, even with the moon still bright? As if paralyzed, we waited and shivered in the cold until the moon went to sleep. Then we stepped into the shallow water and crossed our Rubicon.

The moment we climbed the banks of the opposite shore, all my accumulated tension evaporated. I felt like singing, laughing and jumping around in pure joy. But Jano grabbed me by the leg of my pants and pulled me down whispering,

"Hold it, Gyuri, hold it! This is still Communist country. The West is miles away."

He was right. We had escaped from one totalitarian country but had entered another, although a slightly less cruel one.

Under cover of darkness, we crept cautiously forward stopping almost every minute to look and listen before taking a few more steps. It was quiet, with only the crickets chirping. After a few hours of slow progress, we felt far enough from the border to succumb to the temptation of a huge haystack. We dug into it, made a cozy nest to sleep in and pulled the straw back over us. Through little gaps we could observe the world beyond but nobody could see in.

In the morning we woke still sleepy and very hungry. Luckily, scavenging for food during those early autumn days was not difficult. The fallen fruit under trees could keep us going for a few days.

Changing money was trickier. The possession of foreign currency was a crime in Czechoslovakia, just as it was in Hungary. We had no Czech Crowns, yet we needed some for train tickets and in case we had to bribe our way out of trouble. Going to a bank was out of the question. We had to find a black marketeer and strike a deal with him, but how to spot one? Approach the wrong guy and you would get more for your money than a little change. Again we sought our solution in church.

It was Monday morning. The church was almost deserted. We knelt in an empty pew and observed the few women murmuring their rosaries. They were very old, bent and beaten by a long life of hard work. One, however, was younger and not dressed in black like the others. She looked very much alive. I crossed my fingers, put all my faith in my intuition and approached her after she had finished her prayers.

Gambling that she wouldn't denounce us, I told her our true story and our need to change money. Like so many people living near the border, she spoke fluent Hungarian. For a long time she just looked at me without saying a word. Seldom did I feel eyes piercing through me as hers did. Finally she said, "Come with me." We entered her courtyard and after locking the gate behind us, she disappeared into the cowshed, returning with a cigar box full of foreign currencies. In a minute we had finished the money business and vanished again into the forest beyond the village.

All that day we marched through the woods, eating half-rotten apples. At night we slept in a haystack again. Next morning we felt we were far enough inland not to arouse suspicion. So we went to a railway station to catch a train to Tarnava, a large city more than a hundred kilometers further west.

On the train we didn't chat, just sat in a corner of the carriage, closed our eyes and pretended to sleep. Once in Tarnava, we headed for the Convent of the Daughters of Divine Love, in the center of the city. I rang the doorbell hoping the good nuns would give us a loaf of bread, or with luck even a sausage. They would certainly not denounce us.

When the big oak door opened a crack and the head of a young nun appeared, I asked to be taken to Mother Superior. Hearing me speak Hungarian, she hesitated a second, then let us step in and quickly closed the door behind us. She took us to a spacious waiting room and excused herself. We had time to look around but didn't dare walk on the polished floors with our dusty boots. Saints and bishops gazed down on us from picture frames hanging on the whitewashed walls. Everything looked and smelled spotlessly clean and ascetic. The straight wooden chairs we sat on added to the sense of austerity.

The rustling of a starched habit signaled the arrival of Mother Superior. She was of average stature, but her face and eyes were those of a person used to command.

"Good day, gentlemen, what can we do for you?" Under the business-like tone of her question were warmth and genuine curiosity.

"Sister, I bring greetings from Budapest." I told her that my own sister, Vica, had been a nun of the same order, until the day the Communists dissolved the religious communities in Hungary. They had confiscated all the buildings and chased the nuns out. The older ones who did not have close family to go to found life very hard thereafter.

We had talked about these events for a while when Mother Superior asked, "Have you had dinner yet, dear brothers?"

"No, Sister, not since three days ago."

"Goodness gracious, why didn't you tell me right away? Here I am chatting while you are suffering from hunger. The Lord forgive me. We shall do something about it immediately. You must also stay the night. The room for visiting priests is empty. You must take it."

We accepted gratefully as she summoned two nuns to show us to our room. Shortly after we finished washing, there was a knock on the door inviting us to the refectory for dinner. The long wooden table, large enough to sit twelve or more people, was set just for the two of us. The meal was exquisite, fit for a bishop. Soup, roast chicken, potatoes, vegetables, fresh bread and dessert. This was certainly better than the half-rotten apples we had scrounged up during the past days.

Our bedroom was bright, with a tall window opening to the back garden. On either side of the window stood two beds made up with the softest down pillows and duvets. White glazed earthenware jugs stood on the washstand with soap and freshly ironed towels. On the bare wall hung a crucifix and under it stood a prayer-stool, the only furniture in the room besides the beds, a table and two chairs. Everything a priest might need was there, but for us the pillows and duvets were the most desirable. When I lay down, the sound of Gregorian chants drifting from the chapel carried me off to a heavenly sleep. That night I didn't want to be anything else but a visiting priest.

At dawn we found our boots sparkling with fresh polish in front of our door. As we prepared to leave, we could not thank Mother Superior and her nuns enough. They accompanied us to the gate chatting and laughing, but the moment the gate opened a strange wind blew away all cheeriness. Everyone became silent as one of them glanced out into the street and whispered, "It is clear, you can go."

We walked away slowly, savoring the warm memory of these few hours. The nuns had given us much, much more than we ever expected. They gave us love. We hoped the Lord would hear our prayers and spare them the fate of their sisters in Budapest.

Our spirits were high, full of optimism. The border was only forty kilometers away, a hike of ten hours at most. We should reach it easily by nightfall. Then we would swim a hundred meters across the Morava river and the first rays of sunshine would find us already in Austria. I could almost smell the aroma of coffee and whipped cream in Vienna.

Well, it didn't work out quite that way.

Leaving the city we ducked into the woods again, but our advance was slow. Every time we heard a dog bark we froze. Was someone coming or was that just a deer jumping? We hid in the bushes and waited till the forest became quiet again. Without maps or a compass we didn't know if we were going around in circles. Our cocky confidence of the morning was long gone by the time the sun had set and the river was still nowhere to be seen.

Lost, scared and without a haystack to crawl into, we spent a miserable night tossing and turning sleeplessly on the bare ground. Nor did the morning bring relief. A cold fog hid the sun, our only means of orientation. Finally late in the afternoon our confused roaming ended when, stumbling onto a paved road, we saw a sign. It showed us to be miles away from where we hoped to be.

What should we do? Carrying on in the fog, we could get lost again. And if we didn't reach the river before dawn we would have to wait in hiding until darkness came. Trying to swim across in daylight in full view of the guards would be suicidal.

It was tempting to return home, to get maps, food and a rest and try to escape again later, better prepared. Demoralized, we had mulled over the alternatives already for the umpteenth time, when Jano threw the ball into my court.

"Gyuri, you choose. I'll stick with you whatever you decide." I asked for ten minutes to think and a promise that he would bear no grudges, whatever the consequences of my choice.

And then, for the first time since we left, I allowed myself to look back. I saw my cozy bed, my brothers and sisters, my motorcycle. I smelled Mother's cooking and I felt Emmy's arms around my neck, how soft her skin was and how sweet her kisses. I was daydreaming, not thinking, when Jano yanked me back to reality.

"Your ten minutes are up. What do we do?"

"We go home," I replied without a trace of hesitation.

What a relief to have reached a decision. It felt as if a wave of energy had hit us. Even the fog seemed to lift. Without wasting a second we jumped up and started towards home, caution becoming a casualty in our great hurry. There would be no more creeping through the woods, no hiding in the bushes. Now that we had turned back, we wanted to get home fast, and thus took the open road. Soldiers were controlling everyone heading west, but they didn't bother us. We were going east.

It was silly, crazy, even stupid to go to the railway terminal in Bratislava and buy postcards as souvenirs of our escapade. But we did. Standing at the newsstand, we were choosing one, rejecting the other and acting rather picky while chatting in Hungarian. Suddenly I felt a tap on my shoulder. I turned. The man wore a brown uniform and had a gun on his belt. I will never forget his words, *"Legitimatio, prossim."* 'Your documents, please.'

My first instinct was to run, but that was hopeless. There were other policemen around to catch us. Our only hope was to use our brains and talk ourselves out of trouble. In a split second, I decided to invent a story crazy enough that he might believe it and let us go. It had to be a far-fetched lie, full of details. People often let themselves be fooled by atrocious lies more easily than by half-truths. I also knew I had to appear calm and casual.

"Yes, of course, Comrade." I handed him the only document I had with me, my university index. This was a hard-covered booklet, the size of a thin pocketbook, containing a dozen pages in which the professors entered the results of our exams. It resembled a passport, with many stamps and my photograph.

He slowly turned the pages back and forth without finding what he was looking for. He was Slovak, but spoke Hungarian to us with only a slight accent.

"What is this?"

"My university documents from Budapest, Comrade."

"I am not interested in those. Show me your Czech papers," he said, visibly annoyed.

"Unfortunately, I have not received them yet. I applied at police headquarters and they told me to come back on Wednesday. They said my case was special; they needed time to check me out."

"So what's so special about you?" The mention of Headquarters seemed to work, the frown left his face.

"See, I'm from a Slovak family," I lied. "I'm really Slovak. My grandparents were from a village up in the Tatras. They had no land; they couldn't make a living. They wanted to emigrate to America, but didn't have enough money for the tickets, so they tried their luck in Hungary. They saved and after a few years they bought a small plot. My grandfather always said Hungarians were lazy; they would rather sell the farm than work it."

"Well, but then why is it that you don't have a Slovak name and you don't speak our language?" I liked this. Slovak had now become "our" language.

"During the first war my father was drafted into a Hungarian regiment. The officers always laughed at him just because his name was Breining. One day he decided enough was enough and changed his name to a Hungarian one, to Balázs. After that he had peace."

"And you never spoke Slovak at home?"

"My grandparents always did, but they died when I was a baby. My parents still understood a bit, but my brothers and I couldn't learn it. In school it was forbidden to speak anything but Hungarian. That was the law."

"Yeah, they're nationalists over there, a bunch of chauvinistic bastards. Look how much better we treat minorities here. They can jabber in their language as much as they like. We are generous to them."

"You sure are, Comrade." I added hastily, "You are very generous, not like them. You know, even at University they gave me trouble, just because I was Slovak. I was born there and spoke only their language, and still they bullied me. I couldn't take it anymore. That's why we left."

"So you quit your studies?"

"No, Comrade, I want to carry on at the Bratislava University. They will take us as soon as we have our police clearance." My answer seemed to satisfy him, because he returned my university index without any further questions.

Silently, I thanked God and all the saints for my miraculous escape, when our policeman turned to Jano.

"Can I see your papers too, please."

Jano handed him the only official-looking thing he had in his pocket, a monthly pass to the Budapest transport system. It had a photograph, many stamps and signatures, and a protective metal frame with a plastic cover. As far as streetcar tickets go this was a very impressive-looking one, but it was just that, a glorified ticket. I was anxious to hear what story Jano would concoct with his meager resources.

"Now what is this?" asked the policeman in amazement.

"M-m, m-my p-pass for the the s-street c-car." Poor Jano stuttered abominably even at the best of times, and when he was nervous hardly a sound came out of him. In these circumstances he also had the strange habit of raising an index finger to his lips as if asking for silence.

"Is this the only paper you have?"

"Y-y-yes, C-c-omrade."

"I'm taking you two to the station for further questioning," and turning to me, he said, "You—I want to see your documents again." When he blew his whistle, two more policemen immediately appeared and the five of us marched out to a police van parked at the curb.

Chapter 22

Jail

As the steel door of the van was slammed shut, every nerve in my body screamed to be free, to be out of there. For a short moment I lost all hope of ever tasting freedom again, but once I managed to calm myself my confidence returned, and from then on I thought of nothing but escape.

Our paddy-wagon clattered on the cobblestoned streets so noisily that the cops in the front cabin couldn't hear our whispering. Jano slid closer to me on the wooden bench and muttered into my ear.

"Listen, Gyuri, we'd better cook up a story about why we came here, or they'll beat the shit out of us for trying to emigrate. We'll be locked up for a year."

My friend was right again. We quickly concocted a story and made sure our lies matched should they question us separately. Hoping to get away with only a couple of months in jail and no beatings, we would pretend to be smugglers of motorcycle parts. Our story was almost ready when the van rattled to a stop, the door swung open, and we were led away to be interrogated.

Prepared for the worst, we stepped into the smoke-filled office where half a dozen policemen lounged idly. I expected they would soon get busy on us with fists and billy clubs, but a soccer game saved us. An international match was being broadcast on the radio and suddenly a very excited reporter shouted, "Goal!" The officers jumped up, cheering and shouting happily. They crowded around the loudspeaker, paying infinitely more attention to the radio than to us. A few quick questions, a bit of scribbling in a report and soon we were out of their way, locked up in a cell. They had believed our smuggling story—we would be spared the thrashing reserved for political prisoners.

Sleep did not come easily that night in the small, cold cell. We had to lie on bare planks with empty stomachs, a blinding light bulb dangling from the ceiling, and a stinking urine bucket in a corner. Looking for a way out was useless; the brick walls didn't even have an opening for air.

In the morning we were transferred to a jail with prisoners from other police stations. Our cell was about the size of a large living room, with small steel-barred windows, wooden platforms along the walls to sit, eat and sleep on, but no mattresses, cushions or blankets. The urine bucket stank even more than the one at the police station.

Some three dozen men were already lying or sitting on the planks when our group entered. They had staked out their territory, leaving no empty space. Silently we surveyed each other, and I could see myself having to sleep on the floor with the bucket as companion when one of the old timers made a small sign, moved over slightly and let me sit down beside him. Thus, one by one, we squeezed together and claimed our own territory. Instinctively, without a word spoken, like-minded men banded together. They were a mixed bag of criminals, political prisoners, some aristocrats, a priest or two, robbers, thieves, smugglers, black-marketeers, and a few accountants who had cheated and had been caught. There was even a guy who had killed his wife in a fit of passion. Jano and I wedged in between the abbot of a famous monastery and a tall Polish guy who hardly ever uttered a word.

Every morning a new batch of prisoners was brought in and the ones who had been sentenced the day before were transported to a penitentiary or labor camp. Soon I started looking forward to the new arrivals, for they broke the monotony with their amazing variety of stories. They taught me the art of picking pockets, explained when and how to burglarize a house or to shortchange a customer and many other useful skills. But I also learned where the Iron Curtain had potential holes and how to fool guards at the border. Prison was an excellent school, with many dedicated teachers, and some of the lessons I learned came in handy later on in my escape.

Guys who were in for the third, fifth, or even tenth time for minor crimes were relaxed. They knew the system and what to expect. Prison had become a regular part of their lives, almost like a home—a place to relax in, to be fed and to plan future mischief with new allies. They didn't seem to regret having committed a crime, only the mistake that had led to their capture. The poor wife-killer, though, seemed to have true remorse, for at night we could hear him sobbing quietly. The rest of us were tense. We didn't know when sentencing would come and how much time we would have to spend behind bars. Talking helped to calm our nerves, and that was about all we could do to pass the days. With time, a kind of brotherhood developed with its own value system. Robbers, burglars, priests and thieves we could trust, but not accountants and notaries. They had cheated and were considered crooks.

One of the accountants reinforced this suspicion early in his stay. Every afternoon for half an hour, we were let out of the cell to march around, two abreast, in the courtyard. All of us longed for these walks. It was wonderful to move and breathe fresh air after the confinement and stench of the cell. It kept us sane. On one particular day, just before our walk, a load of coal was delivered and dumped down a chute in the yard. The person in charge forgot to close the steel lid of the chute. If you tucked your arms close to your body and stepped just a little to the side you would fall through the hole into a basement bunker. With some luck maybe you could tunnel out to a sewer or even to the street. I was contemplating doing just that when the Polish guy walking in front of me stepped right into the opening and disappeared. Apart from Jano and I, only the fellow walking beside the Pole could have seen it happen.

A couple of hours after our outing the accountant suddenly yelled, "Hey, where's the Polack? Has anybody seen him?" When he got only shoulder shrugging as a reply he started banging on the door to call the guards. They never found the Polack, but punished all of us by canceling afternoon walks for the next three days. We didn't beat up the squealer but nobody ever spoke to him anymore. That silence could drive a guy crazy.

Once they brought in a man who belonged in a loony bin rather than a jail. He arrived barefoot, almost naked, wearing only a moth-eaten, old-fashioned bathing suit. Judging by the bulge in his crotch he had enormous balls. He looked us over and nonchalantly asked: "Anybody for a cigarette?" Then, reaching down into his crotch, he pulled out a dozen and distributed them. Next he asked: "Anybody want some bacon?" and he produced a few slices. That's when I smoked my first cigarette, but I skipped the bacon.

This crazy guy, who spoke five languages fluently, played a nasty trick on us the same night. While everybody was sleeping he collected our shoes in a row and, walking down the line, pissed into all of them. We didn't have time to react for he got transferred to a mental hospital, leaving our shoes stinking and wet. I'm convinced the fellow was brilliant and just played the idiot to escape torture and prison for some political offence.

Then there came a man who tried to become a Jew. For a short period, the Czech government allowed some Jewish people to leave the country for Israel, and many Christians wanted to sneak through that loophole with false documents.

To trap these guys, the border guards ordered all the males to pull down their pants and present their penises. Our fellow must have performed a do-it-yourself job—so blue, green and swollen was his pecker—although he blamed the police for doing most of the damage with their rubber truncheons.

Another time, a new inmate managed to sneak in some paper and a pencil and was willing to tear off small scraps in exchange for part of a food ration. We scribbled a few words for our relatives, threw the paper out of the window facing the street and hoped a Good Samaritan would find and forward it. The message had to be something neutral that wouldn't make the police suspicious if the note got into their hands. Relatives would have known at least from the handwriting that we were alive.

Political prisoners lived in constant fear of the savage and arbitrary beatings awaiting them. One man who was overheard criticizing communism got rough treatment. This strong-looking guy walked out tall and erect when he was called. A few hours later the guards brought him back and dumped him on the floor. We carried him to the sleeping platform, for he could not walk. They had beaten the soles of his feet with rubber truncheons until he confessed to whatever charges the police invented. For two days he didn't move. He just moaned as his body went through all the colors of the rainbow. I thanked the Lord for being classified only as a smuggler of motorcycle parts.

After two weeks in that cell, Jano and I were taken to the office. The guard shoved a document in front of us, pointed at the dotted line, and said, "Sign there."

"Comrade, I'm sorry but I cannot read Slovak. What is written there?" I asked politely, and he explained in Hungarian.

"The judge gives you six months in labor camp. After that, we'll hand you over to the Hungarian police. You sign that this is just punishment." This was a blow. We didn't expect such a tough sentence, and the thought of being put into the hands of the Hungarians frightened us. They were known to be worse than the Slovak police. Desperately, I tried to reason.

"But, Comrade, we haven't had a court hearing yet. We didn't even see a judge."

"Don't waste my time, bloody idiot," came the answer. "Are you going to sign now or do you want me to knock out your teeth first?"

This was a convincing argument. We both signed.

Chapter 23

Labor Camp

The policeman, still annoyed that I had dared to ask for a judge, shoved two little sealed parcels across the desk. "Here are your watches and documents. Hand them in at the camp, but don't tamper with the seal or you'll regret it. Watch yourselves, you little bastards." Then without any further niceties, he took us to a van already filled with prisoners all clutching their precious little parcels.

He padlocked the door. For a while nobody said a word, but once the motor revved up, people began exchanging bits and pieces of information concerning our destination and the pieces of the puzzle came together. We would be taken by train to Tabor Novaki, a labor camp in the Carpathian Mountains. As it turned out, the speculations were correct.

In the train I was tempted to yank open a window and jump out, but we were moving much too fast, and when it did stop at a station the sight of submachine guns pointing at us kept me immobilized.

The village of Novaki was in a broad valley in the foot-hills of the Carpathians. The whitewashed houses, the pine forest and a small brook winding through the green mead-ows looked idyllic. A short distance further, however, stood the camps. They consisted of rows and rows of weather-beaten wooden barracks built by the Nazis and now used by the Communists. There was one compound for men and one for women, half a mile apart, each housing about a thousand prisoners. The barbed wire fence and guards walking up and down their perimeters with submachine guns on the ready completed the picture. But I also noticed a few positive signs—there were no bloodhounds or searchlights.

Our first stop was the administration barrack where prisoners had to strip and all their worldly possessions were confiscated as they were issued prison garb and a blanket. We lined up outside the door and shuffled slowly forward while men who had been processed before us came out one by one. "Quick, Jano," I whispered, "take off some of your clothes, quick." As the next fellow emerged from the barrack, we shoved into his arms what we had just shed as well as our precious little parcels. This man, whom we had never seen before, put our stuff under his blanket, glanced at us fleetingly and keeping an unbroken stride, disappeared in the crowd.

When in turn we faced the policemen inside, they became suspicious of our scanty outfit.

"Why are you in shirt sleeves and barefoot in this weather, and where are the sealed envelopes?"

"Comrade," I replied, "it was a hot summer day when we came over the border to buy motorcycle parts. We were returning that same afternoon when they caught us. Shirts and pants were almost too much in that heat. That's all we have."

Did they believe me? I'll never know. It may be that they did not want to start an investigation at the end of their shift and decided to let the matter rest. Later during the night, the fellow who had saved our belongings crept over to us to return everything and we immediately hid them in the straw sacks we were to sleep on. He didn't say a word and disappeared before we could even thank him.

Jano and I were determined to break out at the first

reasonable opportunity, and out there our civilian clothes would be indispensable. I wasn't going to stay a prisoner until the end of our sentence. And there was no way I would tolerate being delivered to the Hungarian police for more punishment. We got into this mess by our stupidity, now we had to get out by our wits.

This prison camp was not a Soviet-type gulag or an Auschwitz. Here the purpose wasn't to liquidate people, but to break down the resistance of those who were suspected of political misdeeds. Nobody froze or starved to death, yet if one tried to escape the guards would shoot without hesitation.

We soon learned the routine, which was the same every day except Sundays. At five in the morning the wailing of sirens chased us out of the barracks. Those who moved fast had time to splash a little cold water on their faces before lining up for the roll call and getting a cup of ersatz coffee and a slice of bread. At six we were marched out to build a road towards the mountains. With pickaxes and sledgehammers swinging, we smashed rocks till they turned to gravel. In this way, a hand-made road was built, inch by sweaty inch.

The guards seemed relaxed, smoking leisurely and fumbling idly with their guns. They didn't need to worry, for any fool trying to run away would have presented an easy target over the open fields. They even let us rest occasionally, as long as we leaned on our shovels and didn't try to sit.

Gypsies played an important role in the camp. The Government locked them up in the hope of teaching them sedentary habits, but they were allowed to visit their families once a month. Thus they became our link to the outside world, smuggling out letters and sneaking in soap, cigarettes and other luxuries. I sold my watch to them, bought a toothbrush and hid the rest of the money in my straw sack.

One day the routine changed. Instead of road-building, some of us were taken to the women's camp to dig holes where searchlights were to be installed. I became excited at the thought of seeing girls again.

What a shock I got when we entered! Most of the women were shorn bald, their hands and nails black from work and their prison outfits hanging loose and filthy on their unkempt bodies. They looked old and as wretched as we did, but it was their shaven heads that killed the last spark of fancy I might have had.

We got down to work digging holes for hydro poles. A group of women watched us keenly. When the pits got shoulder-deep I saw a woman unexpectedly jump in where a man was digging. Hardly a minute passed before the two heads sticking out of the hollow started bobbing up and down rhythmically. The guards just grinned with amusement but didn't stop the action, and when other women noticed this, they in turn ran over and jumped in to join more men.

Having been brought up a strict Catholic, I was shocked, although I found this curious display titillating. Yet while all this was going on I kept my eyes on the guards. Were they sufficiently distracted by this mass fornication to let me sneak away and climb through the barbed wire fence unobserved? I was seriously weighing my chances when they apparently got bored watching the orgy and stopped the show with a whistle blow.

Life in camp was bearable. As long as we didn't break the rules or annoy our keepers, we were spared the rubber truncheons and the dreaded solitary confinement. Work was heavy, food rations light, and the drudgery on the road stole every ounce of our energy. After ten hours of labor and a meager supper we dragged ourselves back to the barracks, fell onto our straw sacks and slept till the sirens started wailing at dawn. Sundays were better. There was no work and we could take time to wash and regain our strength.

On the days of rest, people would sit around in small groups talking and telling stories to break the monotony of their lives. They reminisced about their families, their loves, their jobs, their ailments, just about everything that had ever happened to them. Occasionally they switched to singing folksongs. Whenever someone recounted his experiences trying to escape to the West, I always listened carefully.

There was one fellow who, on approaching the border at night, attached a flashlight to a walking cane while he carried a cat in a bag. The moment the soldiers noticed the light they ordered him to stop, which he did. Then, leaving the cane with the flashlight standing, he carefully stepped back and disappeared into the darkness. Furious at being fooled, the soldiers let their dog loose. That is when our man let his cat out of the bag and quietly walked across the border to Austria. But the poor man forgot that he was only in the Russian zone of Austria and he became careless. He was soon caught and shipped back to Czechoslovakia and jail.

Then there was a group of young men who organized a make-believe motorcycle race. They attached racing numbers to their bikes, took off the mufflers, equipped a van with loudspeakers and a big sign painted "Prague-Vienna International Motorcycle Race" and roared off to the border with ear-shattering noise. When the first racer screeched to a halt at the barriers, the loudspeakers began screaming at the guards, "You idiots! We are leading! Do you want the Austrians to win? Open the gate, you bloody fools! You saboteurs!" Confused, the guards hesitated a moment, then hurriedly opened the gate and watched perplexed as the van and a dozen motorcycles zoomed across the border. On the other side, a few of these gutsy guys became careless as well and were later picked up by the police.

Another group of men measured their way across the border, pretending to be surveyors. Carrying a theodolite on a tripod, a long measuring tape, red and white wooden poles, a slide rule, paper and pencils and all the paraphernalia a surveying party needs, they approached the border. At the guardhouse, the leader of the group went directly to the commanding officer, telling him that the border was to be fortified with watchtowers and therefore had to be surveyed. As this was a secret mission they needed the cooperation of the garrison. They were allowed to work undisturbed, measuring distances, heights and angles, writing notes in a logbook while chatting with the unsuspecting soldiers. The moment they reached the border, they threw away all their instruments and ran. But success must have been at the root of their downfall as well, otherwise they wouldn't have been telling their stories in a prison camp.

I listened to dozens of similar anecdotes by people who tried to reach the West but failed. "Be imaginative, brazen, cocky, do the unexpected," they told me. But there was also a warning in their stories. "Be careful once you're over the border, the Russians still control the eastern zone of Austria." I heard the warning loud and clear, but would I always remember?

Five weeks had already passed without a reasonable opportunity to escape. I was getting desperate. Then on a Sunday afternoon as we sat around in small groups chewing the fat, a rumor ran through the camp. On Monday morning the youngest one hundred prisoners would be transported to a coal mine at a new concentration camp. Jano and I would certainly be part of that gang.

"Oh shit," I blurted, turning to my friend. "This is awful. We know this place, we know its layout, the routine, the habits of the guards. There are no dogs, no searchlights. Here we could have a chance, but what can we expect over there? And what do we do with our civilian stuff? If we have to leave it behind, our goose is cooked for good. We might as well give up all hope of ever sniffing the air in America."

Suddenly an enormous anger towards Stalin and all the Communists welled up in me.

"No, you bastards," I swore, "you won't take us anywhere in the morning. We're leaving tonight."

Startled by my outburst, Jano looked at me incredulously,

then his face lit up and grinning from ear to ear he said, "All right, how do we do it?"

The closest we were allowed to the barbed wire was at the latrine, roughly ten meters inside the fence. It was a wooden shack covering a long open pit where a dozen men could squat like sparrows on a telephone wire. Sitting on the beams we could observe the guards through the cracks without creating any suspicion. That is where we decided to escape from at the onset of darkness.

At supper we lined up at the kitchen door, where convicts did the work under the watchful eye of the military. When my turn came to be served soup and bread, I winked at the inmate and said, "Tonight I leave." He looked into my eyes, nodded ever so slightly and scooped a ladleful of meat from the bottom of the kettle. I gobbled down the soup, slipped the meat into my pocket and, breaking the law of the camp, lined up twice more. Jano did the same. Thanks to that gutsy cook we now had some food for the coming days.

It was an unusually warm early November evening. Everyone was out for a last breath of fresh air before turning in for the night. Our barrack was empty. Jano nudged me. "It's time to get dressed."

Unobserved, we slit our straw bags. All the stuff was there untouched, just as we had hid it the night of our arrival—shirts, pants, jackets and money. In a few seconds we stripped, put on civilian clothes and pulled the prison garb over them. We arranged the blankets to look as if someone was sleeping under them. Then with an air of nonchalance we strolled out towards the latrine.

Peeking through the cracks was not as easy as we thought, for we were seldom alone. Men were continuously coming in and out. Some wanted to chat, wondering what we were doing so long in that stench. "Diarrhea, my friend, an awful diarrhea," we groaned.

Around ten o'clock, as men started drifting back to the

barracks, a group began singing old Slovak folksongs not far from the outhouse. Their little choir sounded amazingly good. Once in a while even the guard stopped to enjoy the songs.

"Now is the time," Jano whispered. "He isn't watching. Let's go."

Suddenly my courage left me. I froze, crazy with fear. I saw the guard turn and glance toward the fence, slowly removing the gun from his shoulder. He's going to shoot, I thought, cringing. But he casually slipped the gun onto the other shoulder and turned back to the singers. I was petrified.

"No, Jano, I can't do it. I don't want to get killed. He turns his head, pulls the trigger and it's all over. I can't go. I'm too scared. There must be a safer way. Wait."

He took me by the shoulders, his face close to mine.

"Gyuri, this is our best chance. I'm going. I'll wait five minutes for you on the other side. If you're not there in five minutes, I'll come back for you." I hugged him tight as if for the last time, before he slipped out the door.

A few minutes passed. The guard turned again, left the singers and approached the latrine. My heart stopped. He must have seen Jano, he will shoot. But no, he came in, looked at me, then moved over a few steps and unbuttoned his pants.

After he left I was even more frantic. Time was passing, my five-minute grace was running out. I knew Jano. He always kept his word. The crazy fool would come back for me. He could be killed trying to climb back. To crawl back into a concentration camp was sheer insanity. I couldn't let that happen. Could I live with myself if he came back because of me? But if I went I might get killed. Oh God, please tell me what to do.

It must have been four minutes and fifty-nine seconds when I finally stood up and walked out of the latrine.

Touching the first wire brought me profound peace. I had accepted death. I was ready to die. I didn't even feel the barbs tearing my skin. I felt as if I was gently floating over the fence. It was a delicious feeling, only lightness and peace.

On the other side, Jano jumped into my arms babbling happily. I had to put my hand on his mouth to silence him. But the guard must have heard something, for he began walking rapidly towards us. We threw ourselves on the ground between the reeds and held our breath. He looked around inside the fence, shook his head and continued his beat. We got up, slipped out of our prisoner's jackets and pants and, walking ever so cautiously, left the camp behind.

Once we were far enough from imminent danger, we speeded up. In eight hours of darkness we covered forty kilometers, mostly over fields and meadows. Steering clear of villages, we let dogs, farmers and policemen sleep and dream.

At the six o'clock roll call the guards would discover that we had escaped. By then we had to be far, far away, so we hurried, almost ran, to catch the first train of the morning. As a further precaution we split up, keeping close enough for visual contact, yet sufficiently far that if one of us got into trouble the other could get away.

Since Jano stuttered abominably, it fell upon me to buy the tickets. *"Dva do Pezinok,"* I told the clerk, exhausting my entire Slovak vocabulary. He put two tickets on the counter and mumbled something, which I presumed was the price I had to pay. Giving him the biggest bank note I had, I hoped he wouldn't say a word, just give me change if there was any. He returned a fist full of coins, I nodded approval and walked over to a rickety bench in the waiting room.

My friend observed me from a distance as I slipped one of the tickets under the bench and then ambled out to the tracks. He took my place, retrieved his ticket and boarded at the far end of the coach. Once the train started to move, I closed my eyes and pretended to sleep like a man without a worry in the world. At Pezinok, about thirty kilometers from the border to Austria, we got off and left town separately to join up again in the safety of the woods.

It took us three days and nights of sneaking through forests and fields to get to the border. An excruciatingly slow pace, but we didn't take any chances. At noon on the third day, looking down from a hilltop, we could finally see the Morava river. On the far side, about a kilometer away, puffing rings of smoke and stirring up a cloud of dust, a tractor was plowing Austrian soil.

The river separating us from those distant fields shimmered ever so gently. Only a hundred meters wide after the summer drought, it promised an easy crossing. But that was an illusion. A large gray building surrounded by high stone walls dominated the scene on the Slovak shore—headquarters of the border patrol.

We crouched among the bushes to study the movement of the soldiers. Walking in pairs, they kept watch over the river through binoculars. Sometimes a truckload of soldiers drove along a road that was otherwise empty of all traffic. The guards looked everywhere, but strangely, they didn't pay attention to the stretch of river in front of the garrison. Was it beyond them to imagine that someone could be brazen enough to swim across right under their noses? Maybe. We chose that spot for our crossing. But we knew we had to wait until late in the night, when even the most conscientious guards might nod off a bit.

Around three in the morning, stiff from lying on the barren ground for many hours, we started creeping down to the river. It would have been easy enough to reach the water in complete darkness had we not made a small miscalculation. As it turned out, our path was littered with fallen branches, stones and other obstacles on which we could slip, fall and make noise. We had to crawl very slowly, and there was already a shimmer of light in the east when we arrived at the shore.

This time it was Jano who lost his nerve.

"Gyuri, this is crazy," he said. "It will be daylight before we reach the other shore. The soldiers will use us for target practice. We'll be dead ducks. Let's give it up. It's not worth it. Let's go back. Come on, let's go home."

I knew how he felt. Not so long ago, I was in a similar panic. I let his fear pour out before I replied.

"Jano, listen. At the camp I chickened out, now it's your turn to shit your pants. Don't be ashamed. I understand, it's OK. But look, it's still dark. They won't see us. We have come this far. I won't turn back now. It doesn't matter how risky it is, I'm going. But you must decide for yourself. I can't tell you one way or the other. It's your life."

He hesitated for a few moments and then spoke again,

"I have to leave you, I can't do it. God bless you, my friend."

We shook hands and we hugged. I thanked my buddy for staying with me all this time. I also asked him to tell my parents how far I had gotten. Then we parted.

He turned back towards the bushes. I took off my boots, tied them around my neck and stepped into the river. For a moment the cold water took my breath away, but then I started swimming. I was hardly more than twenty meters from the shore when I heard water splashing behind me. It was Jano. We swam together to Austria.

Chapter 24

Austria

I couldn't have held out much longer in the freezing water, when my feet finally touched soft mud. I looked back to the Slovak shore and in the faint light of early dawn I could see the silhouette of soldiers. We had reached Austria in the nick of time. A few more minutes, a little more light, and our story would have ended right there in the waters of the Morava.

Now I could stand erect in full view of the guards, yet only minutes ago the same men would have shot us like stray dogs. They were not necessarily bad people. They were young conscripts, our age, and perhaps they loathed hunting people as much as we detested being hunted. Possibly they would have preferred playing soccer with us instead. But they had no choice. The soldier who didn't shoot straight could end up blindfolded against the wall himself. They always walked in pairs, keeping an eye on each other lest one should bolt across the border. A short while ago I feared them as vicious murderers, but now, as I stood in the West, untouchable, my feelings suddenly changed. Now I didn't despise these unfortunate fellows, rather I pitied them. It was the men who made them play this crazy game that I hated.

The East was still close enough to shout across, yet everything dear to me had faded out of my reach. When would

I see my parents, brothers, sisters and friends again? Would my new-found freedom outweigh my losses? I hoped so, but I wasn't sure.

My thoughts were drifting off. I was trembling violently from the cold and we had to move before hypothermia drained the last bit of our energy. But Jano wouldn't budge. He just lay face down on the muddy grass as if he wanted to stay there forever. I talked and talked, and still he didn't move. I had to give him a couple of good kicks before he managed to shake off his lethargy and we could leave the shore, remembering well the warnings of prisoners.

"Beware of the Russians, the Soviets still occupy the eastern end of Austria. If they find you, they'll ship you back to Hungary in the first paddy-wagon."

We needed help. Dripping wet, teeth chattering uncontrollably, and having gone days with hardly any food, we needed a Good Samaritan. A priest was always a good person to turn to, as he would never denounce anyone. As we dragged ourselves towards the village church of Marchegg, the Devil, lurking among the trees, spotted us. Sensing an easy catch, he disguised himself in the skin of a peasant and stepped in front of us with tempting promises.

"Ah, I see you boys swam across last night. Lucky you. Not many make it. But you must be hungry and need dry clothes. Come with me, I'll fix you up. You help me a little on my farm, I'll pay you good wages and then you can leave when you are ready."

In our need, his tantalizing words sounded like music from heaven. Mistaking him for an angel of God, we forgot the warnings and followed the peasant. At his house, his wife gave us dry clothes and stuffed us full with ham, bread, butter and all the good stuff we had almost forgotten existed. But this wasn't a free meal, for no sooner had we gulped down the last drop of coffee he ushered us out to his field to harvest sugar beets.

It was back-breaking to pull beets from the earth by hand,

bent over for hours on end. It must have been the fever that clouded our minds, or maybe the promised money was too tempting. I don't know. But foolishly we decided to stick it out for a few more days. On the fourth day, well before sunrise, the peasant shook us awake.

"A policeman is waiting for you in the kitchen."

Shit! The bastard had denounced us. I wanted to kick the hell out of him, but there were more urgent things than revenge. We needed money. On the way out, with the policeman close behind, I asked for our wages.

"You won't need money where you're going," answered the peasant and closed the gate behind us. Now I knew how he got the biggest house in the village.

The policeman escorting us was not a mean-looking fellow, not one of those men who like to play with submachine guns under your nose. He had only a pistol in his holster, and no patrol car. He had to take us by bus.

Jano and I were assigned a bench in the center of the coach while our guard placed himself directly behind us. Once the last passenger was on board, the bus exhaled a huge cloud of smoke and launched itself on the road to Cisternsdorf, a Russian army post. The poor old bus rattled lazily along, wheezing and puffing at the slightest hill. It was a slow trip and the guard must have gotten very bored, for he left his seat and went forward. He faced us from a distance of five or six paces, keeping a close watch on us even as he chatted with the driver. From where he sat he couldn't hear us over the din of the motor.

"Listen," whispered Jano, "there's only one cop. If we jump out and run in different directions, then at least one of us should be able to escape. With luck maybe both."

"And the gun?"

"Well, we just have to take a chance. Do it quickly. Be out before he can pull it from the holster."

I thought about it a moment.

"All right. At the next hill we jump. I'll run to the left, you go to the right. Where do we meet?"

We agreed our contact in Vienna would be the religious order my sister belonged to in Budapest. Then we reclined in our seats and pretended to snooze peacefully.

A couple of minutes later the huffing of the bus became heavier as it negotiated a small incline in a forest. I gave Jano a sign and ran in a flash towards the rear door, with him right behind me. The conductor sitting in the back lunged forward shouting, "Where are you going?" I shoved him out of my way, tore open the door and jumped. As I rolled on the pavement, protecting my head with my hands, I saw Jano flying out of the bus.

Brakes screeched, tires smoked, people screamed and above the bedlam I heard the shouts of the policeman, "Halt! Stop! Stop or I shoot." And then I heard the shots.

I ran. I just ran and ran through the forest until my lungs wanted to burst. I heard more shots but not the whistling of the bullets. He must be shooting at Jano, I thought. He must be after him. I ran until I couldn't anymore. When I stopped, there was absolute silence. In my mind I could still hear those shots blasting viciously. One moment I saw Jano lying in a pool of blood, the next he was running far away from the police. Did he get hit? Was he safe? Was he hurt? Was he alive? But I had to blot Jano out of my mind and think of nothing but my own salvation.

I wiped the blood off my bruised face and hands and tried to get my bearings. In the far distance, a church tower shimmered through the haze and cornfields covered the hills as far as one could see. The dry cornstalks left standing after the harvest could shield me from unwanted eyes. Reaching the far edge of the fields I hid there, spying on the peasants coming and going in the village until the church bells rang and everyone disappeared for lunch in their homes. Then I walked to the church.

When I knocked at the presbytery an elderly priest opened the door with a napkin still around his neck. He seemed annoyed by my unexpected visit at such an hour, but when he saw my wounds and heard my story, he mellowed and took me in. He washed the dried blood from my face, gave me food and a few shillings for train fare, and sent me on my way to Vienna, assuring me that between his village and the capital police checks were few and far between.

The East Terminal where I got off the train was in the Soviet sector of Vienna, as was the convent, our designated meeting place. I went there hoping to find Jano but he hadn't arrived yet. Having gotten there so rapidly myself, I wasn't surprised, just apprehensive. The nuns suggested I seek refuge in a shelter run by the Caritas organization in the American zone and explained how to circumvent Soviet patrols on the way. I followed their instructions, walked a couple of blocks, and as I turned a corner, I saw the flag.

High above, only a few hundred feet away on a shiny white pole, caressed by a gentle breeze, fluttered the American flag. How beautiful it was! I moved closer till my hands touched the pole. I wanted to feel the protection of that flag. There would be no more deportation, jail, police beatings, no knocks on the door in the middle of the night, no rubber truncheons for a careless word. No more fear. Under that flag I was free.

If only Jano were with me. I thought of him with sadness and lingering hope and then continued towards the Caritas shelter.

When I got there, my body caved in from the exhaustion of the past weeks. My legs became stiff, I walked like Charlie Chaplin and I couldn't control my bladder. I was put to bed for three days until my condition improved somewhat, and then I had to leave to make room for people worse off than myself. A nurse gave me the address of a shelter for the homeless in a converted air-raid bunker where a cot and blanket were provided for one shilling a night. Each night a different cot, and I pissed into each of them. Luckily they never identified me as the culprit or I would have been thrown out to sleep under the bridges.

Every day I called the convent inquiring about my friend, but the answer was always, "Sorry, no news." I had almost lost hope of ever seeing him again, when on the ninth evening, as I stood in line to get into the bunker, someone tapped me on the back. It was Jano. He had the happiest grin on his face, although he was just a tattered bag of skin and bones. We laughed and joked for a good while before he told me about his Calvary.

After jumping out of the bus he had run into the forest with the policeman shooting and chasing after him. He stumbled and as he fell his pursuer caught up with him, holding a pistol to his head. The conductor and the driver tied his hands and feet, loaded him on the bus and took him to the Russians. The moment Jano was tied up, the cop started running for me.

The Russians tried to find where I was hiding, but Jano wouldn't tell, even after they beat him. On the morning of the ninth day they threw him out. Whether they wanted to follow him or they just got tired of him, Jano couldn't guess. But not taking any chances, he jumped onto a passing truck, explained his predicament to the driver, and the good fellow drove him all the way to Vienna.

Jano was starved and beaten black and blue, and I stank of urine and could hardly walk, but at last we were together and we were free.

What a delicious feeling! We forgot the aches and pains of our abused bodies as we hung around the streets enjoying the city that was so rich and had suffered much less damage during the war than Budapest. Our eyes caressed luxury goods in the shops: cigars, fur coats, bananas, ballpoint pens, and the scent of perfume instead of stale sweat. I remember standing with my nose pressed against a bakery window shamelessly salivating at cakes piled high with chocolate, whipped cream and never-before-seen tropical fruits.

We mingled with the Sunday crowd pushing strollers and pulling yapping poodles along the parks and promenades. I walked the same streets my grandmother had strolled. I recognized the theaters, churches and palaces she had so fondly recalled from memories of her youth.

But as sweet as freedom was for the soul, our bodies clamored for food. We became regulars at the University where the Swedish Red Cross served free evening meals to students. If we wanted a second meal a day, we had to go somewhere else and pay, and so we went in search of work.

At the railway terminal they hired us to discharge coal for two shillings a ton. We worked in gangs of six men, the same nationalities together. Those who were chummy with the foreman could get their wagons shunted over an unloading chute, where half the car emptied by itself and money came easy. We didn't have connections, so we had to shovel every pound of coal twenty or thirty feet to the chute. Complaining was useless; you just wouldn't be hired the next day. Somehow the wagons of the Austrian gangs regularly ended up closest to the chute. I was pissed off at the time, but in retrospect it was a good lesson in understanding the minority experience.

We could have stayed in Vienna, but I was getting restless. I didn't see a future in this divided city bursting with hordes of refugees. It was beautiful, yet I was getting claustrophobia from having to live in the few western-controlled boroughs surrounded by Russian occupied regions. I started to see Vienna, and with it all of Austria, as a dead-end street. I needed more space, broader horizons, greater opportunities. I had to move on.

Jano had similar feelings. He was attracted by Italy, where he had friends and spoke the language. I was tempted by Switzerland, the best place in postwar Europe, even though the toughest to enter. Our ruminations came to an end when I received news from a distant aunt who lived with her husband in the Swiss canton of St. Gallen. Bábi Néni and Hans Bácsi had offered help, if I could only manage to get to them through all the control zones, borders and assorted obstacles holding back the millions of refugees.

The die was cast. I would try to sneak into Switzerland and Jano to Italy. We would explore ways of entering these countries, while keeping in contact through an old classmate of ours, Zebi, who had settled in Bregenz, in the western corner of Austria.

Money, or rather the lack of it, was still our immediate problem. The few shillings earned shoveling coal were barely enough to keep us warm and fed. We needed more before striking out for the unknown. That's when I suddenly remembered my father's parting words. "In Vienna you can go to the Chairman of the Kreditanstalt Bankverein, the biggest bank of Austria. Just tell him you're my son."

I was reluctant to go on what I felt was a begging mission, yet I had to swallow my pride. My pants torn, my collar black with coal, unshaven and smelling to high heaven, I entered the marble foyer brightly lit by crystal chandeliers. The receptionist jumped from his mahogany desk, ready to throw me out, but I spoke the magic words, "The Chairman is expecting me. I am the son of Pál Balázs."

Clicking heels, humble apologies, and I was led higher and higher, over ever-deepening Persian rugs, to the inner sanctuary of the Bank. The Director, an impeccably dressed middle-aged gentleman, welcomed me most cordially. He offered me a seat, summoned a servant with coffee and then inquired about my father. He spoke of my father warmly, of what a fine courageous man he was, of how he had saved the lives of many Jews, how fair he had been to his workers and how brilliantly he had managed the textile firm the bank owned before the Communists nationalized it.

The Director was interested in my escape as well. He invited me to meet his family at supper the next day and then gave me an envelope, saying, "Please, take this. This is the least we could do for your father." I thanked him for his generosity as I left, but words were inadequate to express my feelings for his kindness. He gave me money without making me feel a beggar and showed me a side of my father I had so little appreciated in the past. It was wonderful to hear somebody who knew him well praise the man whom I loved, but whom I knew so little.

I split the money with Jano and we started preparing our departure from Vienna. The thought of playing hide-and-seek with Russian, American, British and French occupation forces while walking all the way to the Swiss border didn't appeal to me. But to ride the train in safety for the seven hundred kilometers, I would have to get hold of an Austrian identity card, a kind of internal passport. In this delicate business, the underworld was more than happy to help when I met my contact in a smoky café.

"Give me your photograph and two hundred shillings, and meet me here tomorrow at the same time. I'll bring you the documents," said the man as he left, while I wondered whether I would see him again.

But his word was as good as gold, and he was already waiting when I returned the next day.

"This is an original identity card," he smirked. "It used to belong to an Austrian. I steamed the guy's picture out and glued yours in. Look how well the stamp matches. Nobody can see that it's doctored. There's only one little problem. The fellow was blond and a few inches shorter than you, so pull a hat down over your ears and hunch a bit when you stand. And remember, you have to remove the picture and mail the card back to me as soon as you reach the French zone. I'll need it for the next customer."

We closed the deal with a handshake like honorable businessmen. I slipped the stolen pass into my pocket and went in search of an old hat with feather and trinkets to match my incarnation as an Austrian salesman.

On the train, with my fancy hat and new identity, I pretended to read the news in the Wiener Courier with the greatest nonchalance. But I could hardly keep the paper from shaking in my hands as the train slowed to a halt an hour later at the crossing of the Enns River. Beyond the bridge was American-controlled territory. Here was the last chance for the Russians to catch me or any other refugee, so they were going to search the passengers thoroughly.

The moment we stopped, soldiers came on board with submachine guns. They checked everybody meticulously, and dragged a few unfortunate people off the train. When my turn came, the soldier seemed to spend an inordinate amount of time studying me. He looked at my picture, then stared at me and again scrutinized the photograph. He repeated the process several times and then lifting my chin with a finger, he turned my head left and right and took a last look before returning the identification card and moving on to the next person.

I didn't dare let out a sigh of relief. Trying not to show any emotion, I just picked up the paper with a bored look and pretended to read while praying for the train to move on. The search seemed to last an eternity, but maybe it was just half an hour before someone blew a whistle and we crossed the bridge for the American inspection.

A lone soldier came on board, with Military Police printed on his white helmet. He stood at the door commanding crisply, "All people illegally on this train raise your hands." I almost lifted my arm, but then thought better of it and kept sitting on my hands. When not a single finger moved in the entire coach, the soldier wished the passengers a nice day and signaled to the conductor, "All clear, move on."

I had entered a new world indeed.

Chapter 25

Switzerland

Austria chopped up among the Allies into four occupation zones had not been for me. I hadn't had much luck with the people. A peasant had denounced us to the Russians, which almost cost us our lives. Later we were cheated out of our wages at the railway yard where we shoveled coal. There were just too many refugees from Eastern Europe, the Austrians were fed up with us, and we with them.

In Switzerland my relatives had been anxiously awaiting me for a while. Hans Bácsi, who was a born Swiss citizen, had lived a long time in Hungary, where he had met and married Bábi Néni, a distant aunt of mine. During the war, as the Russian Army approached Hungary, this childless couple had left everything behind and fled to Switzerland. Hans Bácsi was an agronomist and now managed one of the largest Swiss farms. I was determined to go to them. Maybe I could settle there as well.

My friend, Zebi, who had escaped from Hungary earlier than I, was working in Bregenz, a border town between Austria and Switzerland, and he knew a lot about what to do and not to do when sneaking into Switzerland. I spent a few days with him before attempting what I hoped would be my last illegal border crossing. Zebi and I went over the plan very carefully, for this time I had to do more than hide and run.

"The frontier is the Rhine," he said, "but there is a spot where a small piece of Austria extends to the far shore. You should take the bridge leading there. Once across, immediately get off the road, turn left and disappear into the forest straddling the border. You'll find a wire fence blocking your way. Climb over it and you'll be in Switzerland. Is this clear so far?"

"You mean there's more?"

"Sure is. That was the easy part. Now listen carefully. The Swiss accept only refugees who came from the East non-stop. People who have already received Austrian residence permits are sent back immediately. You have your permit. Destroy it. Invent some lies to explain how you got here. But watch out. Once you get rid of your Austrian documents, should an Austrian border guard catch you, you're in trouble. You'll be locked up in jail. But if you got this far, you'll make the rest. Anyway, they don't shoot people here, unless they resist."

I waited for nightfall and headed for the bridge in the light drizzle of late December. There was not much traffic, only two or three people and the odd car crossing over the Rhine. When I got to the middle of the bridge, I reached into my pocket for my Austrian residence permit. I was ready to flick it into the river when a man appeared a short distance away. Oh shit, it's a policeman, I thought, and my hand froze. As he got closer I wanted to turn and run. But he was only a drunk making his way home. I tore up the permit and threw the shreds over the railing.

The familiar feeling of being a nobody, a hunted animal, grabbed me immediately. Don't screw up now, I told myself, a few more steps and you'll be over the fence.

"Halt, Polizei!" commanded a firm voice as a flashlight shone in my face. The voice had an unmistakable Swiss German accent. I was in Switzerland.

"Come with me to the police station, please." I had never heard the word *please* from the mouth of a policeman. It gave me a clue as to how I was to behave during questioning. There would be no rubber truncheons, no brutality. This was to be a battle of wits.

At the station, he took his time writing down my name, date of birth and nationality, then he looked straight into my eyes and asked, "Now tell me, how did you get here from Hungary?"

The moment of truth had arrived. I thought, if I blink, if my voice falters, if I show any hesitation, I am lost. I must tell my story calmly. Not too fast. Relaxed, as if I were talking to a good friend.

"I came by train directly from Budapest," I lied.

"Then you have an Austrian visa."

"No, sir, I didn't ride inside the train. I tied myself to the underside of the coach."

"What, you hung under a wagon for twelve hours?"

"No, sir, I didn't hang. I put a wooden plank between the springs and the axles. That's where I rested. You can't see it from the outside."

The cat and mouse game went on for an hour or more. After a while I almost forgot where I was. I started to believe my own story. I saw all the greasy nuts and bolts and felt the rattling of that virtual train as it sped along, my head only inches away from its spinning wheels.

"Then why did you get off at Bregenz? Why didn't you ride it all the way to Switzerland?"

"Sir, I just couldn't hang on anymore. Not for a minute. My fingers were numb from the cold. I was slipping down under the wheels."

"All right. Do you have any relatives in Switzerland?"

I told him about Hans Bácsi and Bábi Néni. He telephoned

them and when he heard they would take me in and guarantee my good behavior, the interrogation was over. I could go to them once the official paperwork was issued.

In the meantime they put me up in a refugee camp. I lay down on one of the bunks and fell asleep. Outside, the first snowflakes of the winter began to turn the world sparkling white.

Chapter 26

Come to Canada

On the farm we worked from sunrise well into the twilight, as harvest time was approaching. It was hard work, but I enjoyed feeling healthier and stronger and seeing my muscles grow. I was also becoming more skillful. Six months before, trying to plow, I had zigzagged like a drunkard on the fields with my team of young horses to the great merriment of the other farmhands. But now I could plow a furrow just as straight as any man around. Nobody laughed at me anymore. I had earned their respect. The men were a great bunch, hard but fair, and full of jokes and laughter. Best of all was the loving warmth of Hans Bácsi's and Bábi Néni's home.

It was a great life but for one thing: I didn't want to become a farmer. Since childhood I had known that when I grew up I would become an engineer, and I wasn't going to give up that dream. On the farm I would have had to save my meagre wages for years to afford the Technical University in Zurich. Refugees were not allowed to work in higher-paid jobs in those days. I had to leave war-torn Europe and try my luck in a country where refugees were welcome.

Australia, New Zealand, Canada, South Africa or Argentina, any country would do, as long as they accepted immigrants and offered decent jobs. I wrote letters for help to never-seen relatives and friends, and to their friends and uncles. A few people answered, but the kindest reply came from Canada. Nick, a school buddy of mine from Budapest, was now studying at the University of Toronto. He wrote:

"Come to Canada. It's a great country. It's huge and empty. There are only two people and a moose per square mile. Plenty of room for you. I'll get you a scholarship from the University of Toronto, and then you can apply for a student visa. I can also lend you a few dollars to help with the ship fare."

This sounded great. I immediately fell in love with Canada, although I knew nothing about it. Only Quebec City was on my mental map, placed there by Churchill and Roosevelt when they had met at the Citadel during the war. I even recalled seeing a news photo, showing people in big fur coats tobogganing on the boardwalk at the Château Frontenac. But I had never heard of Toronto. I borrowed an encyclopedia to learn more about this weird country where a bear was supposed to lurk behind every second tree and the snow melted only for a few weeks in July.

Nick lived up to his promises. A few months after his reply, the University of Toronto sent me a letter granting a bursary. I applied for a visa the same day.

For a week or two I was in ecstasy. In my fantasy, I could already hear the prairie dogs whistling at me while I hobnobbed with the natives. I was so happy, I didn't even mind cleaning the pig sties anymore. Then, suddenly, the earth began to slide under my feet. A second letter from the university announced the coming of a professor to check out the English knowledge of all those receiving scholarships. Mr. Lynch would want to see me in two weeks time.

This was very bad news. My English hovered around absolute zero. In desperation, I borrowed a grammar book from the village school and began to cram. "This is Jane. This is John. Jane has a ball. John has a book." I knew my case was hopeless, but I wasn't going to give up without trying.

On the appointed day, I knocked on Mr. Lynch's hotel door. He was a tall, slim, well-dressed gentleman and when I greeted him with, "What do you do, Mr. Lynch?" he smiled and my confidence rose a notch. But then he said something, and I became lost in the forest of his words. For a moment I thought of informing him about the comings and goings of Jane and John, but still hoping for a miracle, I decided to keep quiet.

Mr. Lynch was also well-versed in body language and so we understood each other. I have never seen anybody express "Sorry" so eloquently with hands and facial mimicry as he did while revoking my scholarship. I believe he was truly disappointed for having to do it. As for me, I landed in the deepest of all emotional pits.

What should I do next? If the Embassy found out my bursary was canceled, they would refuse to issue my visa. But I wasn't letting Canada reject me, now that I had fallen in love with her. I absolutely had to toboggan at the Château Frontenac and see the caribou run in the wild. I was determined to succeed as I went back to the village library to exchange the English grammar book for one on ships and seamanship. I was already preparing to stow away on a freighter.

Fortunately in the bureaucratic jungle of the Embassy they never noticed that the letter granting me a scholarship had become null and void. They called me in and as the consul stamped my refugee pass with the words "Valid for nine months, gainful employment not permitted," I was in heaven again. I had my visa. I could go. Nine months didn't seem very long, but I knew that somehow, by hook or by crook, I could stretch that, maybe to last a lifetime. And about that gainful employment condition, I wasn't going to worry until I reached the far shore of the Atlantic. Now I had to buy a berth on a ship and everything else would fall into place.

At the travel bureau they suggested a Cunard ship sailing from London-Tilburry to Quebec City a few weeks later. "It is inexpensive," the clerk said, "but you must sign a paper that you will not complain about service and accommodation." Of course I signed. Many people survived even slave ships. Slowly, one by one, I counted out 164 one dollar bills, each representing a day's wages. The balance left in my pocket was the same as the day I had arrived in Switzerland: just about zero. But I had a pass, a visa and a ticket in my hand for a new beginning.

Chapter 27

The Pope and I

Before leaving for England and Canada, there was still one thing I badly wanted to do—visit Italy. Pope Pius XII had declared 1950 as the Holy Year and humanity flocked to Rome for his special benediction. I wanted to be part of that crowd. I had to see the Pope. I had to receive his blessing.

Since it was late summer, there was much work to be done on the farm. Nevertheless Herr Kuehn, our strict yet kindly foreman, let me go under the condition that I return within a week. I stuffed a loaf of bread into one pocket, a big piece of chocolate in the other, stood out on the highway, and lifted my thumb.

When I got to Rome, together with zillions of other pilgrims, I was guided to a tent city that had been set up in the hills beyond. Friendships developed instantly, as there was a common bond: we all had come to get the Pope's blessing.

Sunday was the day we all waited for. I left early to get a good place in St. Peter's Basilica. The crowd was squeezed so tightly inside the church and on the huge square, one could hardly move. Only a narrow passage was kept open for the Pope by a row of priests. While waiting, I had time to look around and admire the majesty of the Basilica, the works of Bellini, of Michelangelo and all the art of a rich and powerful Church. I was happy and proud to be a member of it.

When the crowd suddenly roared *"Il Papa, il Papa!"* I got up on the tip of my toes, hoping to see the simple man walk among the crowd, smiling, touching the people, caressing little children and offering words of joy and blessing in the name of Christ.

But wait. What was this? Pius XII was not walking among the faithful. No, he was carried above their heads on a gilded throne by four liveried men. He sat stiff on purple cushions, dressed all in white from his slippers to his robe and his pointy bishop's hat, all in white except for the sumptuous gold embroidery.

He didn't smile. I detected no warmth in his ashen gray face half-hidden behind steel-rimmed glasses. He turned slowly to the right and left as if moved by clockwork, and with two fingers held together he kept whispering the same words of blessing over and over.

I was shocked. What I was seeing was so far from my expectations that I forgot to kneel until someone pulled my jacket from behind. Suddenly all the marble and gold became foreign to me. Is this what Christ wanted his church to become? Is that man on the gilded throne really the messenger of God? Had Jesus been nailed to the cross with golden spikes?

I didn't know what to do with all these contradictions, but I felt a small crack in the fortress of my faith. Only a minuscule crack, but it would grow with time until eventually the entire edifice would come crashing down.

After the passing of the Pope and the end of the high mass the crowd slowly dispersed, and I went to explore the Forum, Caracalla's Baths and numerous other monuments I had learned about in school. By the time I got to the Coliseum it was already dark.

It was a clear night. The full moon threw a silvery veil over the stones as I walked through the arches, climbing higher and higher until I reached the top row of seats. I was alone. Even the throbbing of the city couldn't reach me through the massive walls. I closed my eyes and people began to crowd in, wearing togas and jostling merrily in expectation of blood and games. Suddenly a roar went up from a thousand throats: Nero was carried in on a golden throne on the shoulders of four legionnaires. He wore only white and gold. Then the games started and the Emperor by the flick of his thumb meted out life or death. A shiver went through me. Had I not seen this man today already? I chased away that sinful thought.

Then the Christians were brought in. "Deny your Jesus and I'll grant you life," yelled Nero. But none did. They sang hymns to the Lord as the lions tore flesh from their dying bodies. I opened my eyes and suddenly I was alone again in the stillness of the night. I asked myself if I would have had the courage and faith of those early Christians. No, I had to admit to myself. I would have rejected Jesus even though he died for me on the cross. I felt ashamed of my cowardliness, but at least I was honest with myself.

After a few more hours of ambling through this marvelous city, I had to head home. At the Swiss border I got off the train and began hitchhiking again. Initially it was slow going, but then a woman picked me up. She was maybe ten or twelve years older than I, perhaps thirty-five. Judging by the car she drove, the elegant dress, the pearl necklace and Piaget watch she wore, she was well-to-do. I sank into the soft leather upholstery, enjoyed the ride and the fragrance of her perfume. I learned her name was Helen. We relaxed, chatting about a million things, when suddenly she said,

"It's well past noon, I'm hungry. There's a lovely restaurant in the next village. May I invite you for lunch?"

I accepted her offer eagerly. I was starved. The restaurant was indeed charming and the food delicious. We had been chatting for a long while, when she pointed to the window.

"Look, it will soon start raining. I'd hate to see you get wet on the road. Why don't you stay at my place? The children are in summer camp and my husband has left for Venezuela on business."

I felt the blood rush to my face, the hair stand up on my legs. As her perfume drifted over to me, every cell in my body desired her. This was the moment to fulfill my dreams—to be in the arms of a beautiful woman, to love, to learn, to experience. But I couldn't accept. That would have been a mortal sin. The Pope said so; he knows; he is infallible. The Church threatened eternal hellfire for crimes smaller than that. The Lord would punish me in Hell.

But I could confess my guilt. After all, they like repentant sinners in Heaven more than righteous ones. Yes, I'd go with her. I'd sin and confess. Then I could sin some more and just keep confessing and confessing.

But that's not why God sent his Son to be crucified. I couldn't play yo-yo with God.

I had no sense of how long I mulled over these thoughts—seconds, minutes, I didn't know. When I looked up she was still smiling softly, expectantly, as I burst out:

"Helen, you are so wonderful. I wish I could accept your kindness, but I have to be back at the farm before nightfall," and I felt my face turning even deeper purple.

She reached over the table, patted my hand and said,

"You're such a sweet, innocent boy. Stay the way you are. There aren't many left like you."

She rose, paid the waiter, and we left. As she was getting into her car temptation began to torment me again. What if the Pope is wrong? What if he isn't infallible? Did God put desire into our hearts just to tempt and then punish us? That would be cruel, and God can't be cruel. What if God is generous but the Pope just doesn't get it?"

I started to run after her Jaguar. I didn't want to be an

innocent, sweet boy anymore. But it was too late. The tail-lights of the car had disappeared in the distance and the cool drops of rain took care of the rest.

Chapter 28

London

I got off the ferry in Dover on a gorgeous September day in 1950. With forty-eight hours to spend in England before my ship departed for Canada, I wasn't about to lose a single precious second of that time. I wanted to take in London, to breathe it, taste it, feel it and see all its marvels.

I walked for hours: Piccadilly Circus, Trafalgar Square, Pall Mall. All the streets I had known by name, I now stood on with my own feet. The same streets where Churchill walked, the place where kings had been decapitated. London oozed history from every cobblestone. And I puzzled: why did people queue instead of pushing and shoving, why did double-decker buses not capsize, why was a penny bigger than a sixpence?

After a while, I needed to rest my feet, so I ambled over to Hyde Park to lie down on the grass. In a corner of the park, people were huddled around a dozen animated speakers. These orators shouted about salvation, damnation, lower taxes, no taxes, free love and a multitude of remedies for all the ills of humanity. The crowd was densest in front of a black man standing on a rickety chair, yelling, screaming and flailing his enormous fists. People cheered him on as he cursed Parliament, the government, the King and all the

British rascals who exploited his Jamaican countrymen. A few people laughed.

I couldn't believe what I was witnessing. Freedom of speech was fine, but wasn't this going too far? I thought, this man must be out of his mind. One couldn't criticize the government this blatantly. They wouldn't tolerate such foolishness. Police would surely arrest the entire rebellious gang any minute. I'd better get away quick.

But there were no sirens, no storm troopers, no tear gas. There was only a sole bobby walking leisurely, his hands behind his back, as if he hadn't noticed a thing. I was shocked. How could he tolerate this seditious activity? I looked at him more closely and then I understood: Aha, he had no gun. Unarmed as he was, no wonder the poor bobby had to pretend he had seen no evil. But how could a society exist without armed police? Why would people obey the law? I had never seen a thing like this. I was convinced England would soon collapse in chaos.

By this time it was getting dark and drizzly. I had to find a bed for the night. The only place in all of Britain where I knew I could find a bunk free of charge was in the insane asylum, for, as luck would have it, my old schoolmate, Gerry, was working there as a male nurse. He offered to smuggle me in and share his small room and cot.

I arrived in front of the hospital, whose turreted, soot-soaked walls resembled more my jail in Bratislava then a place of healing and charity. Shivering and wet, I walked up and down, checking my watch every few minutes. Suddenly, like a ghost floating out of the fog, Gerry stood before me. We hugged, happy to find each other so far from home. Then Gerry explained the strategy.

"I'll walk to the gatehouse. The guard usually sits behind the window in his cubicle. He'll slide the window open, ask for my pass, and then push a button to open the gate. From where he's sitting, he can't see the pavement, so get down on your hands and knees and crawl beside me like a little dog. Do you get it?"

"Yes," I whispered.

"All right then, let's go."

And so, in less then a minute, I found myself in the company of forlorn people, shuffling around in their pea-green gowns, drooling and murmuring to themselves. Most paid little attention to me, but one came to check me out.

"And who might you be, if I may ask, Milord?"

Gerry nudged me, whispering:

"He's Wellington. You can be anyone you like but Napoleon. The old boy is very touchy about that. And by the way," Gerry continued, "you can move around freely during the night shift, my colleague knows about you. But don't show your face during the day. If the supervisor sees you, I'll be fired. Oh, and one more thing, when you go to the toilet, don't close the door behind you. It can only be opened from the outside and only by a nurse."

Having given me all this advice, he took me to his cubbyhole. I lay down on his bunk as he left to start his night shift. He promised to take me around London and show me the sights next day.

It took me a while to fall asleep in the cold and damp room. I was too cheap to feed the fireplace with a tuppence for half an hour's worth of gas. At dawn, still groggy with sleep, I meandered over to the toilet. In the cubicle, I turned my back to the door and was about to start my business when I heard a click.

"Oh no, this can't be. I didn't do it!" But I had. I tried gently to push the door, but it didn't budge. Oh well, Gerry would come and rescue me soon, I consoled myself as I sat down. I waited and waited, but there was no Gerry. I didn't dare make any noise, so I just counted the hours ticking away. Buckingham Palace, Westminster Abbey, St. Paul's and all the sights of London floated by my dreaming eyes, but when I opened them only graffiti stared at me from the peeling paint.

I must have dozed off leaning on the water tank, when I finally heard a key turn in the lock. It was Gerry.

"What are you doing here?" he grinned without any sign of sympathy. "Are you trying to beat the Guinness book of records? Sorry, chum, somebody beat you to it already." He then explained his delay in saving me: seeing the empty bed, he had lain down for a few minutes and fallen asleep. When he awakened the supervisor was already making his rounds, so my rescue had to wait till the evening.

My precious time in London was up. My ship wouldn't wait for me. I had to go. Sneaking towards the outside gate, I took my canine position at Gerry's feet as I had on my way in. Passing the guardhouse, I had a tremendous urge to lift my head and bark at the watchman like a real dog, but I resisted.

Out in the open we laughed, joked and said goodbye.

"Well, you didn't exactly get a Cook's tour of the city. Come again and I'll smuggle you into the Savoy."

"That's a deal," I replied and still laughing about my silliness, I turned and ran towards my ship and Canada.

Chapter 29

Crossing to Canada

The ship waiting at the dock was getting ready for the ocean, her chimneys belching thick acid smoke from her coal-fired belly. She was very old, her rusty rivets showing her age. The peeling paint almost obliterated her name, but one could still read *"SAMARIA."* A seaman took my ticket and pointed to a steel door.

"Go down there, down to the bottom, that's where you'll find your fucking cabin." He was a short, stocky fellow, with powerful shoulders, hands like a gorilla's and a deep but long-healed gash on his forehead. He seemed to have gone through a lot in life, although he couldn't have been much older than I. Handing me back my ticket, he scrutinized me and asked, "Where are you from?"

"Budapest."

"Dann du sprichst Deutsch?" and as I nodded, he continued in a mixture of English and broken German.

"I tried to bomb the shit out of you bastards in Budapest, but the fuckin' Krauts shot us down before we got to you. You're a hell of a lucky bastard, my friend. My parachute landed in an open field and the Kraut put me in a bloody prisoner camp. That's where my German is from."

He grinned, showing no grudges for having missed his

chance of killing me. I felt that for some reason he even took to me as we started telling war stories. Tony was a real Cockney, crude, tough, but with a kind heart, as I later found out. As I picked up my cardboard suitcase he gave me good advice.

"Take the upper berth, or some bugger may puke on you at night. And take your shoes up with you. You need anything, let me know. I'll be around."

I went down deep into the bowels of the ship, amused by our chat and pleased that I now had my own fucking English teacher. I threw my belongings onto an empty upper bunk and looked around. Thirty men were stacked on triple bunk beds snoring, farting and sweating. A small fan was trying to suck out the stench of unwashed men, but the job was just too big. It rattled, threw sparks and then quietly gave up the struggle. We each spoke a different tongue—Ukrainian, Polish, Yiddish, Croat, German, Hungarian, Rumanian—like the refugees of Babel, dispersed and in search of a new home. On the promenade decks people spoke English. I'd have to learn their language fast, I decided, then I could bask with them in the sunshine as well.

Tony told me this was the *Samaria's* last trip. If she made it to Quebec City, then the next stop would be the scrap yard. As she creaked and twisted through an Atlantic gale, I wondered if her rusty rivets would hold for a while longer or whether she would take a shortcut via the bottom of the sea. But she struggled heroically across over ten slow days.

At the London docks I had noticed two automobiles being loaded on board ship. I wanted to know more about those cars. Again I went to Tony, whom I found chipping rust off a winch.

"Tony, do you know who owns those two cars? Maybe one of them would give me a ride to Toronto."

"I don't know," he said, "but I could fuckin' well find it out by tomorrow." And he did.

One belonged to a family with six children. They were obviously unsuitable candidates for my project. The other car, however, was owned by a Jesuit priest from Detroit. Tony pointed out the man as he was walking the deck reading his breviary. Once he had finished his prayers, I approached this tall priest, whose face radiated kindness. He would be glad to take me along, he said, and deliver me to my friends in Toronto. Can one be luckier than this? I asked myself.

On the eighth day the seas calmed down and we sighted land. I was horrified. This couldn't be Canada! Somebody was playing a joke on me. These unending piles of barren rock, devoid of forests, fields and humans could never become my home. I wanted urgently to turn the ship around and go back to Europe. A girl was leaning on the railing all wrapped up in sweaters. Laughing at my fright, she said:

"Relax, that's only Labrador. It will get much better further on."

I didn't know if I should believe her, but she was very attractive and that compensated for the desolate landscape. At that moment, as if ashamed of the land He had created, God pulled a curtain of fog in front of us and everything disappeared. I couldn't guess at that time that many years later I would return to this same coast over and over again in my own sailboat to enjoy the savage beauty of that forsaken land.

Two days later the ship stopped tooting and bellowing and the fog lifted. The country we were now passing through was truly magnificent: Les Éboulements, Murray Bay and finally the Château Frontenac high above our heads. I could hardly wait to step ashore and explore my new country. It was October 8th, 1950, a radiant, crystal clear fall day.

Chapter 30

On to Toronto

Soon after we got off the ship, Father John drove us to a little restaurant—a greasy spoon, he called it. Canadian shock number two was waiting for me here. The place smelled of rancid fat. The table was covered with a sticky plastic sheet that a waitress with red varnish chipping from her well-chewed nails wiped for us. The rag she used, like her grease-splattered blouse, was dirty. No white tablecloth and Swiss cleanliness anymore. This country is filthy, I thought. But an even bigger shock awaited me when I opened the menu: "Hot dogs, all dressed" was the first item. I quickly snapped the menu closed, not wanting to know whether Canadians ate their cats hot or cold, dressed or naked, and asked Father John to order something decent for me.

Next we drove up to the Plains of Abraham. The green of the grass contrasted with the reds, oranges and yellows of the maple foliage under a cloudless blue sky. I had never seen such a gorgeous explosion of color in nature. I walked around in awe as Father John sat himself on a bench and began to read his breviary. Then I ventured further onto Grande Allée looking at the neat houses and well-kept gardens, surprised that there were no fences anywhere. What, no fences between neighbors? They must be good people living in this country, I thought. I'll stay in Canada.

Father John closed his well-worn breviary, stretched his back with noticeable pleasure and said "O.K., I'm finished, now we'll drive to the Grand Seminary where we'll sleep tonight." As soon as I set eyes on the Seminary it was clear to me how it had earned its name. It was grand, well-proportioned and very imposing—a gray building that didn't invite you to play around within its hallowed walls, yet the moment I put my nose through its doors I felt at home. It was the smell. Whether this unique scent came from the incense of the chapel, the wax of the floors or the perspiration of frustrated novices, I didn't know, but the place smelled exactly like the residence of my Cistercian teachers in Budapest.

How comforting it was to feel something familiar in this world of novelty so different from everything I had known before. My new country both excited and intimidated me. Next morning after a good sleep and an early mass sung in Latin, followed by pancakes, eggs and a hot cup of coffee, I was ready to conquer the universe.

The drive to Toronto would take us two days. The only road leading west wound its way through villages on the North Shore of the St. Lawrence River. We shared this narrow highway with buses, tractors, bicycles, yapping dogs and the occasional horse-cart slowly ambling along with a mountain of hay. I didn't mind the slowness, it gave me a chance to take in the country in its fullness and my saintly chauffeur seemed happy as well, as he drove with a calmness befitting a Buddhist monk. We were crawling behind a horse-drawn wagon for some time when Father John asked:

"Can you drive?" Thinking that he referred to horses I proudly replied, "Yes, sir."

"OK, then take over please, I'm falling asleep." For a moment I thought of telling him that while I could rein in a horse with ease, I had never taken the wheel of a car. But my pride was stronger than my good sense and we changed places.

"You're a bit rusty, aren't you?" He remarked as I let out

the clutch and the Chevy jerked forward in leaps. After I managed to avoid a number of oncoming trucks, my good priest fell asleep as if he had full confidence in his guardian angel.

Everything was all right until the wagon in front of us turned off to a side road and the highway became clear. Scared as I was, I just kept the speed as before—five miles an hour to be exact. Behind me the traffic jam extended for miles, twisting and turning like a crazed snake unable to pass in the curves and hills. After a while I couldn't bear the cacophony of honking that had reached a crescendo. I took a deep breath, offered my soul to the Lord and pushed the stick from first into second gear. What a surprise—the clutch didn't burn, the gears kept all their teeth and Father John continued snoring. Let's do it again, I thought, and switched to third gear, this time as smooth as a dream. I swept the drops off my sweaty face and relaxed in my seat as the cars stopped their infernal honking. Only twenty-four hours in this country and I have already learned to drive, I mused with satisfaction. Not a bad place, this Canada.

Mentally I was prepared to see many interesting things: mighty rivers, thousands of lakes, enormous open countryside, but it was the little everyday objects that caught me by surprise. Nothing had prepared me for the first juke-box I saw during a restaurant stop. I was fascinated by these gaudy machines, blinking red, green and yellow lights, full of levers, gears and buttons that manipulated the record of your choice. I couldn't resist dropping in one nickel after another to make the monster blast out what I took for folk-songs. To this day "Cindy, Oh Cindy…" and "Jezebel it was you…" are tunes that are truly Canadian for me.

Then there was the pinball machine, another marvel of North American culture and a gobbler of my nickels. Restaurants were full of amazing never-before-seen stuff: sugar bowls with metal tops and floppy covers, spring-loaded paper napkin dispensers, soda fountains bubbling strange colored liquids night and day, ketchup bottles that, depending on their mood, didn't give you a drop or dumped half their contents on your plate.

Everything was big—the cars, the bridges, the portions of restaurant food—but the biggest were the freight trains. A hundred wagons hitched to monstrous locomotives, blasting away with a deep gurgling roar instead of the high-pitched whistle of dainty little European trains. This indeed was not just a new country, this was a different continent.

By late afternoon we passed through Montreal. Sherbrooke Street was like a tunnel through a forest, the elms and maples arching over the mansions of the rich and powerful. Today the trees are cut, the sumptuous homes have given way to nondescript highrises and many an industrialist has migrated to Toronto or Calgary.

As evening approached and it was time for Father John to read his breviary, I was treated again to something new: a motel. A marvelous invention, I thought, and the price even better—one dollar for the two of us, which we split half and half.

It took another full day to reach Toronto. The old Highway #2 led us along the rapids of the St. Lawrence River that have since disappeared underneath the Seaway. The Thousand Islands were in full glory in their autumn colors as we drove towards Lake Ontario. A magnificent drive, which can no longer be enjoyed today when rushing along the new Highway 401.

It was twilight when we found the house where Nick Makay and his mother lived. What a reception I got! She took me in her arms, kissing and hugging me like a lost son. We spent hours telling our respective adventures from Budapest to Toronto. When finally late that night I lay down to sleep, I knew I had arrived in my new homeland.

Chapter 31

Mr. Ramsey

The house my friends lived in belonged to the Ramseys, a well-to-do elderly couple who had left it unattended in the past while they spent the winter in Florida. Like a magnet, their empty mansion had attracted burglars, forcing them to rent out the place while absent.

They met Nick, his mother and his friend, Tamás, who had all come to Toronto to study and were looking for a home during the university semesters. It was a perfect match. One family moved out in October, while the other moved in. In the spring the game was reversed. By coincidence, it was on a day when both families were in the house that Father John dropped me off at the door. Here I found my long lost buddy and, by a stroke of luck, also met Mr. Ramsey.

The morning of their departure, Mrs. Ramsey was still scurrying around furiously packing boxes and suitcases. Mr. Ramsey, on the other hand, was taking it easy. Sitting in his rocking chair, he was chatting leisurely with Nick. From the occasional glances they threw in my direction, I knew they were talking about me, so I joined them and Nick translated.

"Mr. Ramsey is wondering what you'll do. You can't study yet, you don't speak English and you have no money."

I didn't have any answer, so remained silent. They talked on and Nick told me the essence of their conversation.

"Mr. Ramsey thinks you should get a job, save money and learn English, then go back to your studies."

Mighty good idea, I thought, but that wasn't possible. I showed them my international refugee pass. There in the center, under the Canada stamp, was written in big bold letters, "Student Visa. Valid for nine months. No gainful employment permitted." The last sentence underlined.

That didn't seem to impress Mr. Ramsey. He flipped his hand as if chasing away a mosquito.

"Bureaucrats," he said. "What a bunch of stupid people. Why shouldn't you work?" For a moment he seemed annoyed, but then he turned to me and quietly said, "Come with me." I helped him as he struggled to put his frail body into a camel hair coat that reached down to his ankles. He stopped for a moment to light a cigar, suckling on it with joyous slurping sounds like a newborn babe at his mother's breast. When the fire caught and the smoke was to his satisfaction he beamed happily, took me by the elbow and led me out to the driveway.

I had no idea where he was taking me, yet I knew something good would come of it. I trusted him from the moment we had met the day before. His lively, smiling eyes that looked deep into mine told me this wizened old man was a very smart and kind gentleman.

He would prove me right more than once.

Just now I didn't care what happened next. We couldn't converse, but the ride in his yellow Cadillac was simply too good for me to be worrying about my studies or work. I sank into the soft leather cushions as we floated over endless miles on Bloor Street.

Suddenly I had to laugh. What a change a few days can bring! Two weeks ago I had to crawl on hands and knees into one of London's lunatic asylums to find a bunk for the night.

Now a millionaire was driving me around in his limousine and I could live in his mansion.

I marvelled at how small, sometimes unconnected events can change the course of life. I would never have met my benefactor had burglars not stolen a few suits from his cupboard two years before. Then I laughed again, wondering if Rex, Mr. Ramsey's fox-terrier, would impact on my future as well. Little did I know that one day this cute little dog would indeed make a difference in my life.

My ramblings came to a sudden halt when the car stopped in front of a modest industrial building. The crisp sign contrasted sharply with the faded red brick of the walls. Ramsey Construction it announced proudly.

The pea-green office was small, with only a desk and a chair for the foreman and a few stools for visitors. Along the wall stood a drafting board with a pile of blueprints carefully rolled up, a gray metal filing cabinet and a dozen hard hats hanging from pegs. Most of the space was taken up by shovels, pickaxes and sledgehammers, all well worn but clean and neatly stacked. The man who worked there was obviously a tidy, well-organized person.

"Mike," Mr. Ramsey said to the foreman, "this is George. He'll be working for us. Same pay as the other unskilled ones, ninety cents an hour. No special treatment just because I brought him here." I didn't catch half of what he said, but in an osmosis-like way English words began to penetrate my brain and I understood.

A perplexed look crossed the foreman's face. He studied me carefully. There was even a hint of hesitation in his eye. But finally he smiled and said, "OK, Boss. He seems alright."

Then he motioned me to come closer and with the tip of a pencil pointed at the number seven on his wristwatch and said, "Tomorrow at seven you start." Then to make sure that I understood, he showed me seven fingers.

This was only my fourth day in the country and I was already well on my way to doing something illegal. Back in the Cadillac, I began to worry about breaking the law and ending up in jail. My fear of police was still with me. But watching Mr. Ramsey puffing on his cigar with heavenly calm, I started to relax. This, after all, was Canada, a million miles from everything I had known before. Next morning well before sunrise, I took the tram, still remembering what an old Swiss farmer had told me before I left his country:

"In America time is money. You'll have to work much harder over there."

To be sure I was on time, I arrived at the construction site an hour ahead of everyone. At seven, a dump truck pulled up to be filled with sand. My mates leisurely picked up shovels and without the least bit of rush got down to work. I thought of the old farmer's advice and began to shovel fast, even faster than I used to in Switzerland.

When they saw me, the others dropped their tools and stared in amazement. Finally one of them tapped me on the shoulder and said in a mixture of Ukrainian, Polish and a touch of English,

"No, Comrade, no good, you not in old country. Here we shovel, take it easy," and showed me the Canadian way of doing things. Well, when in Rome shovel like the Romans, I decided, and with great pleasure adjusted myself to the rhythm of my new country.

I liked construction. It was not too hard, even when the temperature dropped below freezing. My fellow workers were a jovial bunch of guys, but there was one enormous drawback they always spoke Ukrainian. My English was getting nowhere. I had to do something about it. So early in 1951, after a few months on the job, I quit, determined to learn something more useful than a hodge-podge of Slavic languages.

Soon Spring had arrived and the Ramseys returned from

Florida, while Nick and his mother moved away. I had to get out of the house as well. Meanwhile, my friend, Gerry, who had been living in England for the past year, decided to immigrate to Canada. I lent him the ship's fare and he came. We rented a room and moved in together.

Shortly after Mr. Ramsey had settled back into his home, I went over to thank him again for his kindness and explain why I left his company. He found my experiences amusing and agreed it was good to switch from learning Ukrainian to English.

Then in a more serious vein he asked, "Tell me, are you a landed immigrant now?"

"No, I'm here only as a student. My visa will expire in a few days. They could deport me any time. I don't even dare to look for a job."

"Hmm" was his only response, as he lit a cigar. He fumbled with his lighter, then stood up with a determined look and took me out to the Cadillac.

"Well, let's see what we can do about your little problem," he laughed, turning on the ignition.

This time we drove to the Immigration Department. A few minutes of waiting, then we were face to face with a middle-aged gentleman in crisp blue uniform wearing the Canadian emblem on his shoulder.

"Good afternoon, Gentlemen. What can I do for you?"

Mr. Ramsey explained my situation in a few words and proceeded to describe my character.

Wow, what a fantastic fellow he's talking about, I thought, struggling not to blush. My own mother couldn't have given a more glowing report.

In closing, he said, "This young man will do honor to our country. We need people like him in Canada. I strongly recommend you admit him as an immigrant."

The officer took off his eyeglasses, searched my face and

put a few simple questions to me. Then he asked me to step outside for a minute. When I was invited back in, he had a signed document in front of him.

"Mr. Ramsey has vouched for you. Therefore, in the name of His Majesty's Government, I declare you a landed immigrant. In five years time you can apply for citizenship." He stamped my refugee pass and wished me good luck, and then we left.

I was still in a daze when Mr. Ramsey dropped me off in front of my new digs. I thanked him profusely, but he only said, "Ah, don't mention it. Anyway, I had nothing much to do this afternoon."

This was Mr. Ramsey. I never had a chance to see him again.

Chapter 32

Job Hunting

I was poring over the want ads in the *Toronto Star* early-one morning, when my eye was caught by the figure of $1.65 per hour. An astronomical sum for a fellow just a few months off the immigrant boat in 1950.

"Hey, Gerry," I called over to my friend, still lazing in our five-dollar-a-week common bed, "What the hell is a break-press? They're looking for an experienced operator."

"Never heard of it," he grumbled. "Look it up in the dictionary and go for it. If you don't know, just bullshit you way through. You have lots of experience in that department."

Thanks for the good advice, I thought, as he rolled over to his other side and I opened our borrowed dictionary.

Webster's had a lot on "break," like destroy, annihilate, slow down and a million more meanings. Same with the word "press," which could represent just as many exotic things. I never found the two words together, however, not even hyphenated. I couldn't guess what a break-press was, but the pay was irresistible and therefore I went to apply. I was determined to operate that thing and to hell with experience.

After nearly an hour-long ride along King Street, the tram finally dropped me at its terminal among dilapidated old brick buildings. I found the address, went in, and there I saw them. There were five of them. Huge, green antediluvian monsters, their nostrils hissing clouds of smoke, their teeth ripping and tormenting sheet metal into forms that looked like garage doors. Beside them the men in hard hats, leather aprons and goggles looked like frightened pigmies dancing in front of a blood-crazed dinosaur.

A sixth machine stood idle, nobody around it. So that's the one they need my help for, I thought, when a giant of a foreman emerged from his glass cubby-hole.

"Guess you came for the ad, young man," he shouted to be heard over the racket. "Show me your hands," and he grabbed my pink hands with his callused paws. He looked at my clean fingernails as if he were inspecting a freak show, then burst out laughing, "No, no, my dear boy, you will never do. I'm sorry, but you have no experience. What do you want to do with these funny things?" and let my hands slip out of his. Then he looked in my face and said, "Try upstairs in the office, they may need a secretary. Good luck," and in parting, gave me a tap on the shoulder.

At the office they were sorry, really sorry, but they had no position open for a unilingual Hungarian secretary at that moment. I should apply again once my English was better, maybe next year.

I found Canadians so funny. Why were they so sorry every time they turned me down? I would have been absolutely useless for these jobs. In Hungary they would have literally kicked me out and thrown a telephone book after me for good measure. Maybe the English were not that sorry at all, just more civilized.

Back in our one-bed-one-chair room, Gerry greeted me all excited, waving the *Star* under my nose,

"Here's the ideal job for you, Gyuri! Canada Packers is looking for experienced slaughterers."

"Sure, sure, Gerry," I said. "That bloody experience business will kill me. Everybody wants you to have experience. How is one to get it if you can't even get through the front door?"

"But, man, you have experience! You cut the throat and plucked the chickens every time your mother needed one. You even slaughtered a cow after the war. Go for it, my friend. You'll succeed."

Gerry's confidence in me was making me mad. It was easy for him to be cocky, he had already landed a good job cleaning floors and toilets in a hospital.

I was tired of this wild goose chase, but my desire to have some money and a bed of my own won the upper hand. So I went to Canada Packers. The personnel manager listened carefully as I explained to him how to wield a knife in the chicken coop. He seemed even more interested as I illustrated with hands and feet how I dismantled a cow with an axe. When he opened his mouth, I knew immediately that he was a born Canadian. The "Sorry, but...." gave him away.

By this time I had blown my last penny on streetcar tickets and was exhausted from the long walk back to our digs. With hands in my pockets and head bent against the cold wind I almost missed the Help Wanted sign in the window of a restaurant. I'll go in and see, I thought. They can throw me out but at least I'll be warm for a few minutes.

I couldn't believe that Mr. Kelly hired me on the spot as a waiter with the fabulous pay of seventy-five cents an hour. Fortunately, this roly-poly man talked and gesticulated so vigorously that I didn't have to say a word. He must have been the most generous Christian, with the softest heart for immigrants. I could even keep my tips and stuff myself full in the kitchen.

My restaurant, the Scot's, was neat, no smell of rancid oil, no chipped Formica or torn leatherette, yet the place was half-empty. The dark and dingy Saint George's next door, on the other hand, was bursting at the seams. I decided to do my utmost to help reverse that situation, to pay back Mr. Kelly for his kindness.

My first customer landed on my long row of empty stools only half an hour after I took my position behind the counter. "Beautiful day, sir, a beautiful day," I informed him while he shook water from his Macintosh and used half a dozen paper napkins to wipe his rain-soaked hair. He looked at me as if he had never seen a fool before. But that was all I had to offer. Other meteorological conditions were not part of my vocabulary yet and, after all, one should have a sunny outlook on life.

Luckily he ordered something we call by the same name all over the world, coffee. Milk or cream, white or brown sugar presented slightly more interesting linguistic challenges, but we managed to sort that out as well. As he prepared to leave I assured him again that this was a beautiful day. He just smiled and slid a coin under the empty cup.

For me this was a beautiful day indeed.

My challenge was not only the lack of English, but also the great array of unknown food—Cornflakes, Jell-O, dough-nuts, Seven-up, banana splits and many more that I had never seen or heard of before. One day, two bobby-socked girls giggled their way in and wanted to have a "Chocolate Sunday." I tried to explain to them that it was only Saturday, but they wouldn't listen and left in a huff.

They were like the fellow who ordered two eggs and then said something about sunny-side. I was happy to find a common ground of interest, since Gerry and I lived kitty-corner from the Sunny-side Amusement Park. So I con-veyed this information to him, albeit with some difficulty. He didn't quite get it at first, so I repeated it several times. When he started to mention Christ and a number of other heavenly personalities, I got really confused. Luckily the cook knew his business and sent me back with two regular fried eggs. For several days afterward, I wondered what was up at Sunny-side.

Then a lady of somewhat faded beauty fluttered in. The red varnish chipping off her nails, brown hair showing under old peroxide, but most of all, the aroma she exuded were not signs of high society.

"Give me a roast," she ordered curtly.

Feeling sorry for the poor woman, I had the cook cut an extra slice of beef and add double portions of gravy, turnips and potato. I was really proud of myself as I put the heavy plate in front of her. She looked at that huge pile of food, then furtively at me and then back again to the plate. Finally she pierced me with angry eyes and exploded.

"What the hell is this?"

"The roast you ordered, madam," I stuttered.

"I ordered a toast, you..." and she rattled of a litany of words, none of which, I presumed, were very flattering to my intelligence.

"Pst, pst," I muttered, anxiously glancing towards the cash where Mr. Kelly was adding up receipts. "You lady eat roast, I charge toast."

Now it was her turn to be perplexed. She looked at me with fluttering eyes and wide-open mouth. She glanced cautiously at Mr. Kelly who was still distracted and then, giving me a conspiratorial grin, she attacked the roast. I even made her a toast so that she could wipe up the last drop of gravy.

When she had finished and let a discrete, unladylike burp escape, she opened her purse for me. There was only fifteen cents in there, the price for a coffee and toast, but nothing for a tip. "Sorry about that," she said, "but that's all I have," and left to pay.

I gazed after her for a moment, happy that finally I could be generous to someone in this huge country. I was pleased even though I knew that my kindness came from Mr. Kelly's pocket.

I had soldiered on for over a week behind the counter,

feeling more and more at home among the little glass cups of wiggly Jell-O, when Mr. Kelly handed me my pay envelope.

"I'm sorry, George," he said, "but I had to choose between keeping my restaurant or you, and I chose the restaurant. Learn some English and come back next year. You'll make a good waiter one day." I shook his hand gratefully. He had given me a chance. From now on it should go easier, I thought, and I walked over to Saint George's. Let's see if they could use an experienced dishwasher.

Chapter 33

I Become an Engineer

Jobs kept running through my fingers like slippery fish, but eventually a fantastic one landed in my net. The Ontario Research Foundation hired me in April 1951 as a technician in the wire rope research lab. A year earlier, an elevator cable had broken in a Nova Scotia coal-mine, sending a dozen men to their death. In the hope that such tragedies could be avoided in the future, the Foundation was developing a technology to warn of cable weakness. The work involved electronics, mechanics, chemistry the stuff engineers feed on. And to my delight, everyone spoke only English. I learned fast. In a few months I was ready to return to my studies.

And so one day in August, ten months after I had arrived in Canada, I walked to the Engineering Department of the University of Toronto to see the Dean, Professor Allcot. I caught up with him in a corridor as he was hurrying from one lecture to the next. When I told him why I needed to see him he glanced at his watch and said, "OK. I still have a few minutes. Come to my office."

There he leafed through the mangled remains of my Hungarian university documents salvaged from jail, labor camp and a multitude of other mishaps. He pointed to one thing and another and asked me to translate into English.

"Well, the curriculum in your country looks similar to

ours," he remarked. "Where would you like to start?"

"The third year," I replied without hesitation. "I did the first two in Budapest. I don't want to lose time by repeating a year, Sir."

"Good for you," he said. "Great if you make it. But if you fail, the money you lose will be your own." He sent me to the Registrar's office to enroll. Ten minutes later, I emerged from those hallowed halls bewildered by the ease and speed with which I had become a student again.

Now, where to find money? Attending lectures while keeping a day-time job would be impossible. So let's try a student loan, I thought, and went to the purser's office. The lady in charge spoke softly yet firmly.

"This is a very difficult course you are taking. Students whose mother tongue is English find it hard to pass. You won't be able to make it. Come back next year and we'll reconsider your application."

Oh! This hurt. 'What, me not making it? I'll show you, my dear lady,' I fumed inwardly, as I thanked her politely for the advice and left.

But I still needed something to live on, so I started a part-time business making souvenirs for homesick Hungarian immigrants. I took photographs of old picture postcards from Budapest, made enlargements and printed lots of copies. Ödön Kristoffy, who immigrated to Canada before me, lent me tools and his basement to fabricate wooden frames. On Sunday all the female members of his family piled into my twenty-five dollar jalopy and we headed to the Hungarian churches for our sales campaign. We set up a rickety card table on the sidewalk, stacked our merchandise high and waited nervously for people to stream out at the end of the service.

"Hungarian souvenirs! Beautiful Hungarian souvenirs!" I yelled, the moment the first unsuspecting worshipper appeared at the door. "Mementos from our beloved country!

Only fifty cents a picture! A dollar fifty framed professionally!" I kept shouting as loud as I could.

People came, they looked and they bought. Eszter Kristoffy displayed our wares, her mother wrapped the purchases and her grandmother handled the cash. We had to be fast, for ten minutes later people were heading home and the street was bare. "Quick!" Grandmother cheered us on, as we loaded our gear into the car and zoomed over to the next church for another show.

After a few Sundays of repeat performance, all those who were interested had bought their pictures. The souvenir season was over. I had earned a hundred dollars and could now face life fearlessly for a while anyway.

At university things went fine until winter arrived and I was down to eating mostly baked beans and potatoes. Al, a classmate of mine, was just as broke. Finding no better solution, we signed up for the night shift at Union Station to load freight cars. Unfortunately our hope of making do with a few winks after lectures proved an idle dream. By midnight we were ambling around the rail yard like drunken zombies.

Yet, every problem has its solution. Ours took the form of sleeping cars parked on a spur-line. Taking two-hour turns, we would sneak into one for a snooze. If the foreman was looking for my mate, I told him Al had just gone to the toilet. The moment he turned his back I rushed to the wagon, woke Al and took his bunk. Still, try as hard as we could, it became impossible to juggle studies, exams and a night shift very much longer.

Luckily the Christmas season was approaching and department stores needed extra help. Eaton's must have been desperate for salesmen, because they hired me for the afternoon shift in the leather goods department to sell lady's alligator-skin handbags. I was very proud when, after two weeks of earnest effort, I finally managed to sell one. My customer, an elegantly dressed gentleman, paid a price that must have covered all my wages and still left Mr. Eaton grinning happily.

The temptation to slack off in my studies during those weeks became almost irresistible. Yet every time the devil began to lure me I remembered the lady in the purser's office saying, "You won't be able to make it."

"Like Hell I won't," replied my pride and I doubled my effort.

When the school year ended in April 1952 and I got my marks, I went knocking again at the purser's door. She recognized me.

"Ah, there you are. How are things? How's your English coming along?"

I didn't say a word, just handed her my exam results. Her eyes bulged. She shrieked, "My God, this can't be true! You didn't just pass, you made the Dean's honor list. Congratulations! This is wonderful." She was so excited, I thought she might jump up any moment and start kissing me. Instead she did something much more sensible. She granted me a two hundred dollar student loan.

That loan, combined with my savings from summer jobs, was enough to carry me through the last school year in style. The curriculum was easy, the girls lovely and I traded my jalopy for a used car that could be started with the push of a button.

When I graduated in 1953 the demand for engineers was fabulous. Like chickens at a feeding trough, companies scurried to be ahead of the competition in picking up the good graduates.

My first interview was with Bell Telephone Co. They offered a generous salary, gave a detailed job description and spent a lot of time explaining the pension program. "Hey, guys," I thought, "I haven't even started working yet, and you're already talking about retirement. Yours must be a boring company. You're not for me."

Next, a man from the personnel department of Ingersol Rand interviewed me. He introduced himself as a psychologist and handed me several sheets of a questionnaire. The answer to most of these was so obvious that I suspected a trap. I thought I would outwit him by marking the opposite of what appeared to be right. I still remember one of those questions:

"On a Saturday night would you prefer to go dancing with a pretty girl or work on a challenging problem in the laboratory?"

How can anybody ask such a stupid thing of a red-blooded young male? I reasoned, and put the mark at the lab.

When I had finished all one hundred questions he analyzed the results, the furrows on his forehead getting deeper by the minute.

"You seem to be lacking in social skills Mr. Balas." He said. "The tests show that you are ... how shall I say? ... more interested in the abstract than in down-to-earth affairs. In theoretical science, I'm sure you would reach brilliant heights. Unfortunately, we don't have any such positions available in our company. I doubt there is one even in all of Canada. Perhaps you should consider returning to Europe. People are more scientifically inclined over there."

Well, that was the end of my brief encounter with Ingersol Rand. Luckily there were many more firms looking for engineers, but I would never again try to outsmart a psychologist.

At Massey-Ferguson, the interview took place in the opulent Board Room. Bunched together at one end of a long mahogany table sat eight men, all wearing pin-striped, charcoal suits, their faces stern, like a group of executioners. They told me to sit at the head of the table so they could see me better. I became nervous. Thoughts of the Spanish Inquisition came to mind. Question after question hit me like burning irons while my English deserted me altogether. I just stuttered. The men kept glancing at each other; finally, one of them cleared his throat to announce the verdict.

"Mr. Balas, we regret that your speech impediment prevents us from offering you a position. Thank you for having taken the time to apply with us."

Outside, the air smelled fresh under the elm trees. What a relief to be out of there, even without a job.

Then a gentleman from Alcan visited the campus. A faint smile ran over his face as, holding my C.V. in his hand, he remarked,

"I see you live on Indian Road Crescent. Do you, by any chance, know a Mr. Ramsey?"

"Yes, I do. As matter of fact, for a while I stayed in Mr. Ramsey's house."

"That's amazing. Tell me, does he still have his fox-terrier, whatever its name was?"

"Rex," I told him. "A cute little dog. After work I used to take him out for walks in Hyde Park."

We then talked of nothing but dogs. He was particularly interested in the long-haired Hungarian shepherd dog, the Puli. We had been going on merrily for perhaps a quarter of an hour when he said:

"It's been very pleasant chatting with you, but now we have to get down to business. Do you want to join Alcan?"

I didn't know a thing about the outfit I was now invited to join. He didn't speak of a job description or a location, and even less of a salary. Yet I sensed that an organization where people cared for dogs would also care for humans and not just profits. This could be my kind of company. So I closed my eyes, listened to my intuition and jumped on his offer.

At the end of April, I got into my old jalopy and headed northeast. The second day as I crossed the Laurentian Natural Park, still under heavy snow, I started wondering what I had gotten myself into. Were they sending me to the North Pole?

Finally, as I descended from the mountains into the broad

valley of the Saguenay, the scenery became inviting again. In the distance I could see Arvida, a small town, with its immense aluminum smelter. There I would start my new life, work several years as an engineer, create a yacht club and build sailing dinghies with a dozen other young bachelors. And eventually this is where I would meet Louise, the woman who would become my wife.

I had come home.